lonely 🌐 planet

POCKET

SEATTLE

TOP EXPERIENCES • LOCAL LIFE

ROBERT BALKOVICH

Contents

Plan Your Trip   4

Space Needle (p68) SERGEY NOVIKOV / SHUTTERSTOCK ©

Explore Seattle 31

Special Features

Survival Guide 147

COVID-19

We have re-checked every business in this book before publication to ensure that it is still open after the COVID-19 outbreak. However, the economic and social impacts of COVID-19 will continue to be felt long after the outbreak has been contained, and many businesses, services and events referenced in this guide may experience ongoing restrictions. Some businesses may be temporarily closed, have changed their opening hours and services, or require bookings; some unfortunately could have closed permanently. We suggest you check with venues before visiting for the latest information.

Top Experiences

Explore Pike Place Market

Seattle's beating commercial heart. **p34**

Ascend the Space Needle

Seattle's most iconic sight. **p68**

Enjoy Pop Culture at MoPOP

Tactile exhibits explore pop history. **p72**

Discover Fremont's Public Sculptures

Celebrate Seattle's eccentric art scene (pictured: Fremont Troll). **p112**|

Check Out Seattle Art Museum
Small but mighty art temple. **p38**

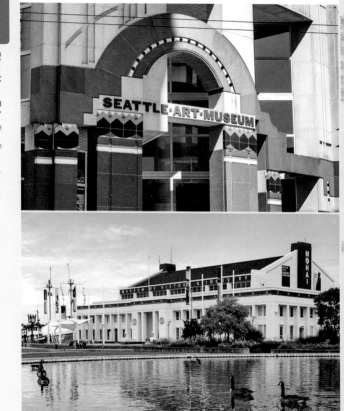

Time Travel at the Museum of History & Industry
Extensive collection of Seattle ephemera. **p86**

NORMAN ONG / SHUTTERSTOCK ©

Dive Into Aviation History at the Museum of Flight
Interactive museum of aerial innovation. **p138**

Glimpse the Past at Pioneer Square
A slice of Seattle's yesteryear. **p54**

Go Wild at Discovery Park
Natural wonders in city limits. **p124**

Reflect on the Artworks at Chihuly Garden & Glass
Shrine to Seattle art royalty. **p70**

Dining Out

DAVID TONELSON / SHUTTERSTOCK ©

Seattle's food scene was always noteworthy, but in recent years it has exploded thanks to the popularity of farm-to-table practices and new American cuisine. As with other major cities you'll also find that immigrant communities have made their mark, as have flighty contemporary dining trends.

Northwest and Pacific Rim Cuisine

A lot of Seattle's gourmet restaurants describe their food as 'Northwest cuisine.' Its cornerstone is high-quality regional ingredients that grow abundantly in Washington State: seafood so fresh it squirms, fat berries freshly plucked, mushrooms dug out of the rich soil and a cornucopia of fruit and vegetables.

Another distinguishing feature is pan-Asian cooking, often referred to as Pacific Rim cuisine or fusion food.

What Seattle Does Well

Surrounded by water, Seattle is an obvious powerhouse of fresh seafood. Local favorites include Dungeness crab, salmon, halibut, oysters, spot prawns and clams.

Other genres in which Seattle excels are bakeries (a by-product of its cafe culture), Japanese food (the sushi is unwaveringly good) and – perhaps surprisingly – spicy Ethiopian food; the bulk of the East African restaurants are in the Central District (CD). The city used to be noted for its dearth of Mexican restaurants, but in the past decade or so many shockingly good ones have opened.

Best Restaurants In Seattle

Sitka & Spruce If you had to sum up Seattle cuisine in three words, this is it. (p105)

La Carta de Oaxaca Unmissable regional Mexican cuisine and the best brunch in town. (p131)

Staple & Fancy It's worth blowing your budget on the

ASSEMBLY / GETTY IMAGES ©

tasting menu at this rustic Italian spot. (p131)

Maneki This traditional Japanese restaurant is a unique dining opportunity in town. (p60)

Best Seafood

Walrus & the Carpenter Ballard oyster bar where they serve 'em raw with white wine. (p132)

Sunfish Head to Alki Beach for some of the best fish-and-chips in the city. (p141)

Pike Place Chowder Pike Place institution where there are always 40 people queuing for four tables. (Pictured above left; p46)

Best Recent Openings

It's been a tough time for new restaurants due to COVID-19, but before the pandemic these were some favorite newcomers on the scene

Heartwood Provisions Fine dining that actually makes a splash on the scene. (p44)

San Fermo A welcome addition to Ballard in one of the neighborhood's oldest buildings. (p132)

Kamonegi The traditional soba noodles and tempura here have shaken up the Fremont dining scene. (p118)

Arthur's Aussie-inspired breakfast and lunch bites sure to keep the bad-weather blues away. (p142)

Restaurant Reservations

Most Seattle restaurants don't require bookings. The hot new places often fill up quickly, though, so if you'd like to eat at one of these, it's best to call ahead or book online to avoid disappointment.

Bar Open

It's hard to complain too much about Seattle's crappy weather in a city where local beer and wine, artful craft cocktails and one-of-a-kind spirits are in such abundance. No doubt about it, Seattle's an inviting place to enjoy a drink, whatever your poison.

Macro Numbers of Microbrews

The microbrew explosion rocked the Northwest around the same time as the gourmet-coffee craze, but not coincidentally: Seattle's Redhook Brewery was co-founded in 1981 by Gordon Bowker, one of the guys who founded Starbucks.

You can find microbrews practically everywhere, but brewpubs often feature signature beers and ales not available anywhere else. Most of the brewpubs offer a taster's selection of the house brews. Pints range in price from $5 to $7, and you can usually get a small sample to try before committing.

Bar Scenes By Neighborhood

Capitol Hill is the place in Seattle for a night out, with gay bars, dive bars, cocktail lounges and themed bars aplenty. Belltown also has a famous bar scene, although it's not as grungy as it once was. Of the city's outer neighborhoods, Ballard and Fremont are a must for beer lovers with old-fashioned pubs sitting alongside boisterous brewpubs and cozy nano-breweries, while the U District is resplendent with dive bars.

Best Brewpubs

Fremont Brewing Company Old-school brewery where you can taste beer at wooden tables on the factory floor. (p119)

Pike Pub & Brewery One of the oldest and most cherished brewpubs in Seattle. (Pictured, p48)

Optimism Brewing Co A newer player on the scene, having been founded in 2013, this is an industrial-

DAVID TONELSON / SHUTTERSTOCK ©

style brewery and tasting room in Capitol Hill. (p107)

Best Whiskey

Westland Distillery Microdistillery with tasting room and the yardstick against which other Seattle whiskeys are measured. (p58)

Bookstore Bar Settle down on a sofa with a book and a glass of the water of life. (p46)

Radiator Whiskey Pike Place bar with a menu exclusively for Manhattans. (p46)

Whisky Bar A change in location hasn't dampened the throat-warming effects of the numerous whiskeys. (p812)

Macleod's Genuine Scottish pub in the bar bonanza of Ballard. (p127)

LGBTIQ+ Bars

Pony Capitol Hill's own agora, located in a renovated auto shop. (p106)

Wildrose Lesbian pub in Capitol Hill. (p107)

R Place The place to watch go-go boys gyrate before trying some moves of your own. (p103)

Outwest Bar A mellow LGBTIQ+ outpost in West Seattle. (p144)

Food & Drink Happy Hours

Most Seattle bars run their happy hour from around 3pm until 6pm. Some offer happy-hour deals on food as well. Latenight happy hours, usually 10pm until 1am, are becoming more common.

Showtime

Quietly aggrieved that it was being bypassed by big-name touring acts in the 1980s, Seattle shut itself away and created its own live-music scene. There are also plenty of other artistic strands, including independent cinema, burlesque theater, bookshop poetry readings and some high-profile opera, classical music and drama.

Live Music

One of the major strengths of Seattle's music scene is its diversity of venues. Here you can attend concerts at a 17,000-capacity arena, midsized bastions of the '90s grunge heyday, neighborhood bars, jazz clubs, and small pubs and cafes that specialize in undiscovered talent.

The Arts

Seattle is a book-loving town and there's a literary event practically every night. The film industry also has national stature.

Theater runs the gamut from nationally recognized productions and touring Broadway shows, to staged readings of obscure texts in cobbled-together venues or coffee shops. The Seattle Symphony has become nationally known and widely respected, primarily through its excellent recordings.

Readings

Maybe it's because of the rain, or maybe it's all that good coffee, but Seattleites read voraciously – whether it's the latest literary novel, an underground comic or a home-stapled zine. A lot of authors live here and there are some important literary landmarks worth checking out.

For detailed event schedules and to find offbeat happenings at nonmajor venues, check listings in the *Stranger* or the *Seattle Weekly* websites or look for events calendars posted in bookstores around town. Most readings and open-mike events are free.

400TMAX / GETTY IMAGES ©

Best Live Music Venues

Neumos The other pillar of Seattle's dynamic scene has updated and remains relevant. (Pictured, p108)

McCaw Hall Go and hear the Seattle Opera raise the roof. (p82)

Chop Suey Diverse selection of live acts, with indie alternating with hip-hop. (p108)

Tractor Tavern The anchor of Ballard's live scene specializes in alt country. (p134-5)

Best For Undiscovered Talent

Espresso Vivace at Brix Hip coffee bar where local bands play regular laid-back sets. (p106)

High Dive Small Fremont dive for up-and-coming bands. (p119)

Nectar Lounge Early promoter of Seattle's now-famous hip-hop scene. (p119)

Owl & Thistle Downtown Irish pub with fine fiddlers and folk music. (p46)

Entertainment Listings

To make sure you're up to date with Seattle's entertainment listings, scour the *Stranger* (www.thestranger.com) or *Seattle Weekly* (www.seattleweekly.com) websites.

Treasure Hunt

Seattle, like any big US city, has a whole range of big-name stores. More precious and of more interest are the one-of-a-kind shops you'll find hidden down alleys and crammed between coffee shops. The city's tour de force is its bookstores and record stores, surely some of the best in the nation.

KAY ROXBY / ALAMY STOCK PHOTO ©

Independent Bookstores

Ironically, the city that spawned Amazon guards one of the best collections of indie bookstores in the US. In 2015 Seattle prepared itself for the ultimate oxymoron when the tech giant opened its first bricks-and-mortar bookstore in the U District (you can give it a miss). With print book sales on the rise for the first time in over a decade, it's proof that bookstores can and will survive.

Viva Vinyl

Vinyl is dead? Think again. Sales have been rising in the US since the mid-2000s. The word on the street is that Seattle has more record stores than any other US city, and with such a weighty musical legacy to call upon, who's arguing? Every neighborhood has its favorite independent dealer; some are encyclopedic, others no bigger than an average student bedroom.

Marijuana

In Seattle adults aged 21 and over may buy up to 1oz of pure weed (or 16oz of solid edibles, or 72oz of liquid product) for private consumption from a licensed seller. The 'bud tenders' who work behind the counter are knowledgeable, chatty and always ready with recommendations and advice. If you're a total novice, just let the staff know. Dispensaries tend to be total judgment-free zones.

COLLEEN MICHAELS / SHUTTERSTOCK ©

Best Bookstores

Elliott Bay Book Company Best bookstore in the nation? Add it to the list of contenders. (Pictured above left; p109)

Ada's Technical Books & Cafe Book specialist in Capitol Hill with beautiful decor and a fine cafe. (p109)

Left Bank Books Just in case you lost your copy of Das Kapital. (p51)

Best Record Stores

Easy Street Records & Café Drink coffee, imbibe beer, eat snacks and...oh... browse excellent records. (p144)

Georgetown Records Rare picture-cover 45s and vintage LPs next door to Fantagraphics comic shop. (Pictured above right; p145)

Singles Going Steady If this name means anything to you, this punkish record shop is your nirvana. (p83)

Best Dispensaries

Origins Cannabis Things are a little bit friendlier in West Seattle, including their dispensaries. (p145)

Ganja Goddess At the time of writing one of the few dispensaries accepting payment by card. (p65)

Taxes & Refunds

A 10.1% sales tax is added to all purchases except food to be prepared for consumption (ie groceries). Unlike the European VAT or Canadian GST, the sales tax is not refundable to tourists.

Outdoors

Never mind the rain – that's why Gore-Tex was invented. When you live this close to the mountains, not to mention all that water and an impressive mélange of parks, it's just criminal not to get outdoors. One of Seattle's greatest assets is that it's a large city that doesn't require you to leave to find outdoor recreation.

On the Water

Seeing Seattle from the water is a surefire way to fall in love with the city. The calmest, safest places to launch a boat are Green Lake, Lake Union or near the water-taxi dock in Seacrest Park in West Seattle. There are many places offering kayak and canoe rentals in these waterfront locales, as well as outfits that do classes and instruction, usually from around $70 per hour.

Hiking

In Seattle, it's possible to hike (or run) wilderness trails without ever leaving the city. Seward Park, east of Georgetown, offers several miles of trails in a remnant of the area's old-growth forest, and an even more extensive network of trails is available in 534-acre Discovery Park, northwest of downtown.

Burke-Gilman Trail

Cutting a leafy, vehicle-free path through multiple north Seattle neighborhoods – including the U District, Fremont, and Ballard – the Burke-Gilman Trail gets busy with human-powered traffic on sunny weekend days, when cyclists overtake joggers, and skaters weave in and out of walkers and strollers.

Best Activities

Discovery Park Get a taste of the Pacific Northwest's great outdoors without leaving Seattle. (p124)

Green Lake Park Where to watch other people puff, pant and pose in their REI gear. (p117)

DARRYL BROOKS / SHUTTERSTOCK ©

REI Tackle the climbing wall in the Northwest's outdoor megastore. (p97)

Best Water Activities

Center for Wooden Boats Go sailing on Lake Union – it's free on Sundays! (Pictured; p92)

Green Lake Boat Rental Take it easy and have fun in a paddleboat on the waters of this calm, sheltered lake. (p117)

Alki Beach Park Swim, splash, windsurf, kayak, paddleboard and get wet in Seattle's substitute California. (p141)

Best Neighborhoods to Get Outdoors

Ballard & Discovery Park Two wild waterside parks to lose yourself in. (p123)

Green Lake & Fremont Running, cycling and boating bonanza around Green Lake and on Fremont's Lake Union waterfront. (p111)

Georgetown & West Seattle There are plenty of opportunities for cycling, kayaking, swimming and long walks on the beach. (p137)

Madrona & Madison Park Lake front parks and miles of trails for walking or running await. (p99)

Golf Courses

Seattle's parks and recreation department (www.cityofseattle.net/parks) operates four public golf courses. You'll also find a couple of private courses. Book ahead; fees start from around $35.

For Kids

Take it easy, overworked parent. Seattle will entertain, pacify and often educate your energetic kid(s) without them even realizing it. Some of the attractions are obvious – a children's theater and a zoo. Others are more serendipitous; don't miss the pinball museum or the exciting urban theater of Pike Place Market.

SVETLANASF / SHUTTERSTOCK ©

Dining with Kids

Most Seattle restaurants are kid-friendly. The only places where you're likely to see 'No Minors' signs is in pubs, gastropubs and dive bars (notwithstanding, many pubs will serve families as long as they don't sit at the bar). Some places introduce a no-kids policy after 10pm.

Pike Place Market has the widest selection of cheap, immediately available food and is a fun place to hang out and eat.

Seattle Center

The Seattle Center has the most concentrated stash of kid-friendly activities in the city. There are several dedicated children's museums and theaters, and many of the general interest museums and sights have an interactive approach that will appeal to youngsters.

Best Kid-Friendly Restaurants

Beecher's Handmade Cheese Kids fall instantly in love with their mac 'n'

cheese cartons. (Pictured above left; p44)

La Vita é Bella A traditional, family-friendly Italian trattoria in Belltown. (p80)

Piroshky Piroshky Adventurous eaters will be satisfied with this Russian bakery's flaky pastries. (p45)

Top Pot Hand-Forged Doughnuts Who doesn't love a good doughnut? (p78)

Best Kid-Friendly Museums

Museum of History & Industry Learn about Seattle's past through interactive exhibits full of tactile

ARTAZUM / SHUTTERSTOCK ©

components and engaging quizzes. (p86)

Seattle Pinball Museum Pay $12 to $15 for unlimited use of several dozen pinball machines. The catch: getting your kid out again! (p58)

Museum of Pop Culture You could fill an afternoon in the Sound Lab alone, where adults and kids can requisition drum kits, guitars and keyboards. (p72)

Museum of Flight There are plenty of interactive exhibits for airplane-obsessed young ones, including a flight simulator. (p138)

Best for Getting Outdoors

Discovery Park Miles of safe trails and beaches for kids to explore. (p124)

Hiram M Chittenden Locks Watch the boats traverse the locks and see the fish ladder. (p130)

Center for Wooden Boats Come for free sailboat rides on Sundays from 10am. First come, first served! (p92)

Alki Beach Park Perfect for sandcastles and beachy picnics. (Pictured above right; p141)

Top Tips for Parents

○ ParentMap (www.parentmap.com) has child- and family-friendly activity listings.

○ Seattle has ultra-steep hills; tricky for strollers and scooters.

○ Most larger stores have change tables.

Under the Radar Seattle

GEORGECOLEPHOTO / SHUTTERSTOCK

Seattle is well known for the Space Needle, artisan coffee and the Pike Place Market. But there are also many lesser-explored corners of the city for adventurous visitors to uncover.

The Central District

East of Capitol Hill, this neighborhood known as the Central District. The historic home of Seattle's Black community, this area doesn't boast much in the way of tourist infrastructure, but the under-sung restaurant scene and opportunities for cultural horizon–broadening make it well worth a visit. Check out the schedule of historic venue Washington Hall (www.facebook.com/ WashingtonHall) if you're looking for any-thing from a concert to a dance performance to a boxing match. Or simply walk the streets and take in the abundance of arresting public graffiti art, making sure to stop for a bite at Fat's Chicken & Waffles or Cafe Selam, one of the neighbourhood's several Ethiopian restaurants.

Washington Park Arboretum

When it comes to outdoor activities, spots like Discovery Park and Lake Union tend to dominate the conversation. Those looking for an alternative should head north from the Central District to Washington Park Arboretum (pictured). This park has miles of trails and you'll be strolling among a collection of majestic trees, from towering sequoias to picturesque Japanese maples. Walk to the far northern end of the park to find a trail that will take you across Foster and Marsh Islands, which are located in Union Bay. Continue and you'll end up in the U District – the perfect place for a post-excursion bite to eat.

Coffee

F11PHOTO / SHUTTERSTOCK ©

Every rainy day in this city is just another opportunity to warm up with a cup of joe. Seattle practically invented modern North American coffee culture, thanks to a small store in Pike Place Market that went global: Starbucks (pictured). But these days that storied chain is just one of dozens vying for attention.

Local Coffee Chains

Unless you fell asleep in 1984 and have just woken up, the word 'Starbucks' needs no elaboration. But Seattle hosts a number of other, smaller coffee 'chainlets,' many of which only have branches in the city and its suburbs. Each has their own unique charms, and some are known for excelling in things like ultrafluffy foam or a particularly friendly atmosphere.

Best Coffee Shops

Zeitgeist Coffee At Zeitgeist it's all about the coffee – and the gorgeous almond croissants. (p63)

Storyville Coffee This place opened in 2013 but quickly established itself as a contender in a crowded marketplace (p47)

Espresso Vivace at Brix Drink coffee, listen to the Ramones, check out the latest street style. (p106)

Milstead & Co Multi-roaster in Fremont choosing the best coffee on the market; menu changes daily. (p119)

Victrola Coffee Roasters When hipsters go to heaven they get teleported to Victrola in Capitol Hill. (p106)

Four Perfect Days

Day 1

Start your day at **Pike Place Market** (p34). Spend the morning getting lost, browsing, tasting, buying and bantering with the producers. Don't miss the **gum wall** (p42) or the Rachel the pig sculpture.

Scamper across Alaskan Way and marvel at the vistas created by the demolition of the viaduct that used to blight this area. Tour the **Aquarium** (pictured above; p43), then allow a good hour to browse the latest exhibits at **Seattle Art Museum** (SAM; p38) on the western edge of downtown.

Head to Pioneer Square for a drink in the amiable sports bar **Fuel** (p64).

Day 2

Head to the Seattle Center. Opt first for the crystallized magnificence of **Chihuly Garden & Glass** (p70), then zip up the adjacent **Space Needle** (p68) for dazzling views.

Walk to the waterfront to enjoy imaginative art at the **Olympic Sculpture Park** (p78) before returning to the Seattle Center for an afternoon of rock-n-roll nostalgia at the **Museum of Pop Culture** (pictured above; p72). Afterwards pop into **Macrina** (p79) for a coffee and perfectly flaky pastry.

In Belltown, hit the **Whisky Bar** (p82) and order a Westland single malt.

RIVERNORTHPHOTOGRAPHY / GETTY IMAGES ©

CHAMOMILE ALYA / SHUTTERSTOCK © ARCHITECT FRANK GEHRY

Day 3

BRENDAN SAINSBURY / LONELY PLANET ©

Wake up with a latte at **Zeitgeist** (p63) in Pioneer Square, possibly the city's best indie coffee shop. Cross the road to visit the entertaining and free **Klondike Gold Rush National Historical Park** (p58).

In the International District, call in on its most famous sight, the **Wing Luke Museum** (p59), and its most esoteric, the **Pinball Museum** (pictured above; p58), before imbibing tea in the **Panama Hotel Tea & Coffee House** (p63). From here head to Capitol Hill.

Warm up on the Pike–Pine corridor with a cocktail on the patio at **Pony** (p106) before heading over to **Optimism Brewing Co** (p107) for a straight-from-the-beer-vat microbrew. End the night with live music at **Neumos** (p108).

Day 4

PAUL CHRISTIAN GORDON / ALAMY STOCK PHOTO ©

Greet the day in South Lake Union, where a lakeside park hosts the **Museum of History & Industry** (p86), a roller-coaster journey through Seattle's past.

Flag a bus to take you to Fremont. Soon after crossing the Fremont Bridge, you'll start to see the neighborhood's many whimsical pieces of public art. Visit the **Theo Chocolate Factory** (pictured above; p115) before you hit the Burke-Gilman Trail to Ballard.

Stroll Ballard Ave to experience the neighborhood's self-contained nightlife. There's the rambunctious **King's Hardware** (p127). Louder still is the **Tractor Tavern** (p134).

Need to Know

For detailed information, see Survival Guide p147

Currency
US dollar ($)

Language
English

Visas
Check www.travel.
state.gov for the latest
visa requirements.

Money
ATMs are widely
available. Credit
and debit cards are
accepted at most
hotels, restaurants and
shops, even for small
transactions.

Cell Phones
The US uses CDMA-
800 and GSM-1900
bands. SIM cards
are relatively easy to
obtain.

Time
Pacific Standard Time
(GMT/UTC minus eight
hours)

Tipping
Tipping is a must-do.

Daily Budget

Budget: Less than $150

Dorm bed in a hostel: $35

Pike Place Market take-out snacks: $3–6

Certain days at museums: free

Public transportation average fare: $2.75

Midrange: $150–300

Online deal at a no-frills hotel: $130–180

Pub, bakery or sandwich-bar meal: around $10

Cheap tickets for sports games: from $12

Short taxi trip: $12–15

Top end: More than $300

Downtown hotel room: more than $250

Meal at trendy Capitol Hill restaurant: from $50

Tickets to the theater or a concert: from $40

Advance Planning

One month before Start looking at options for
car rental, accommodations, tours and train
tickets.

Two weeks before If you're hoping to see
a particular performance or game, whether
it's the Mariners or the opera, it's wise to buy
tickets in advance.

One to two days before Book popular restaurants in advance. Search the *Stranger* and
the *Seattle Times* (p15) for upcoming art and
entertainment listings.

Arriving in Seattle

✈ Sea-Tac International Airport

Ground transportation, including shuttle buses and ride share pick-ups like Uber and Lyft, pick up on the 3rd floor of the airport garage. Link Light Rail also connects the airport to downtown.

King Street Station

Situated in Pioneer Square with good, fast links via bus, streetcar, and train to practically everywhere in the city.

The Piers

Both Pier 91 in the Magnolia neighborhood and Pier 52 in downtown Seattle have bus and shuttle services.

Getting Around

🚌 Bus

Pay as you enter ($2.75/1.50 per adult/child); you'll receive a slip that entitles you to a transfer until the time noted.

🚈 Light-Rail

Regular all-day service between Sea-Tac Airport and the University of Washington via downtown. Fares vary based on destination.

🚋 Streetcar

Fare ($2.25/1.50 per adult/child); buy at station before boarding.

🚢 Water Taxi

Runs between Pier 50 on the waterfront to West Seattle; daily in summer, weekdays only in winter (pictured).

🚕 Taxi

Initial charge $2.60, then $2.50 per mile.

MAX LINDENTHALER / SHUTTERSTOCK ©

Seattle Neighborhoods

Ballard & Discovery Park (p123)
You can commune with nature in Ballard's numerous parks and chink glasses with beer aficionados in its bars and breweries.

Downtown, Pike Place & Waterfront (p33)
Downtown's skyscrapers and department stores temper the brimming energy of one of the US' biggest and oldest farmers markets.

Pioneer Sqare, International District & SoDo (p53)
Seattle's oldest quarter offers handsome historic redbrick buildings and is home to the city's Asian immigrant communities.

Georgetown & West Seattle (p137)
Art, beer and airplane memorabilia light up Georgetown; beaches, retro vinyl and fish 'n' chips illuminate West Seattle.

Discovery Park

Fremont Public Sculptures

Museum of History & Industry

Museum of Pop Culture

Chihuly Garden & Glass

Space Needle

Pike Place Market

Seattle Art Museum

Pioneer Square Architecture

Fremont & Green Lake (p111)
Fremont is off-beat and bizarre and proud of it; Green Lake is prettier but more sober.

Belltown & Seattle Center (p67)
Culinary and musical invention characterize creative Belltown; entertainment venues and museums crowd the Seattle Center.

Queen Anne & Lake Union (p85)
Old money haunts Queen Anne's gracious mansions; new money spurs the rapid development around Lake Union.

Capitol Hill & First Hill (p101)
Capitol Hill is brimming with exciting night life and restaurants, while First Hill's antique architecture dazzles.

Museum of
⦿ Flight

Explore
Seattle

Downtown, Pike Place & Waterfront

Downtown Seattle is a standard (except with more hills) American amalgam of boxy skyscrapers and brand-name shopping opportunities. It is given welcome oomph by Pike Place Market, the city's heart, soul and number-one must-see sight. The waterfront is home to kitschy tourist attractions and incredible Puget Sound views.

The Short List

○ **Pike Place Market (p34)** *Seeing, smelling and tasting the unique energy of this Seattle icon, from the charismatic fish throwers to the creative – but disgusting – gum wall.*

○ **Seattle Art Museum (p38)** *Experiencing the latest surprise lighting up this constantly evolving museum.*

○ **Seattle Great Wheel (p42)** *Viewing Seattle's ongoing waterfront regeneration from inside an enclosed pod on this giant wheel.*

Getting There & Around

🚇 Sound Transit's Central Link light-rail from Sea-Tac Airport has two downtown stations: Westlake, and University St and 3rd Ave.

🚋 Streetcar service to South Lake Union from Westlake.

🚌 You can get downtown easily from any part of Seattle by bus.

Neighborhood Map on p40

Top Experiences 📷
Explore Pike Place Market

A cavalcade of noise, smells, personalities, banter and urban theater sprinkled liberally around a spatially challenged waterside strip, Pike Place Market is Seattle in a bottle. In operation since 1907 and still as soulful today as it was on day one, this wonderfully local experience highlights the city for what it really is: all-embracing, eclectic and proudly unique.

◎ MAP P40, B4

📞 206-682-7453

www.pikeplacemarket.org

85 Pike St

🕐 9am-6pm Mon-Sat, to 5pm Sun

🚇 Westlake

Orientation

If you're coming from downtown, simply walk down Pike St toward the waterfront; you can't miss the huge **Public Market sign** etched against the horizon. Incidentally, the sign and clock, installed in 1927, constituted one of the first pieces of outdoor neon on the West Coast.

Main & North Arcades

The thin, shed-like structures that run along the edge of the hill are the busiest of the market buildings. With banks of fresh produce carefully arranged in artful displays, and fresh fish, crab and other shellfish piled high on ice, this is the real heart of the market. Here you'll see fishmongers tossing salmon back and forth like basketballs. The end of the North Arcade is dedicated to local artisans and craftspeople – products must be handmade to be sold here.

Down Under

As if the levels of the market that are above ground aren't labyrinthine enough, below the Main Arcade are three lower levels called the Down Under. Here you'll find a fabulously eclectic mix of pocket-sized shops, from Indian spice stalls to magician supply shops and vintage magazine and map purveyors.

Economy Market Building

Once a stable for merchants' horses, the Economy Market Building, south of the market entrance, has a wonderful Italian grocery store and one of the oldest apothecaries on the West Coast. Look down at the Economy Market floor and you'll see some of the 46,000 tiles sold to the public in the 1980s for $35 each. If you bought a tile, you'd get your name on it and be proud that you helped save the market. Famous tile owners include *Cat in the Hat* creator Dr Seuss and former US president Ronald Reagan.

★ **Top Tips**

o If you dislike crowds, visit the market early (before 10am).

o Wander over to adjacent Victor Steinbrueck Park for beautiful clear-weather views of Mt Rainier.

o Join a Seattle walking tour; plenty of them start in or around the market and all skillfully explain its history.

✗ **Take a Break**

If you need a seat away from the crowds, sneak into the slightly hidden Alibi Room (p47), a large dive bar off Post Alley that serves excellent pizza.

Carbo-load on some of the city's (maybe the world's?) best mac 'n' cheese at Beecher's Handmade Cheese (p44).

Post Alley

Narrow Post Alley (named for its hitching posts) is lined with shops and restaurants. In Lower Post Alley, beside the market sign, is the **LaSalle Hotel**, which was the first bordello north of Yesler Way. Originally the Outlook Hotel, it was taken over in 1942 by the notorious Nellie Curtis, a woman with 13 aliases and a knack for running suspiciously profitable hotels with thousands of lonely sailors lined up nightly outside the door. The building, rehabbed in 1977, now houses commercial and residential space.

Gum Wall

Seattle's oddest and most unhygienic sight is the bizarre gum wall (p42) situated at the southern end of Post Alley. The once venerable redbrick facade is now covered in used pieces of chewing gum, originally stuck there by bored theater-goers standing in line for a nearby ticket office in the 1990s. Despite early attempts by the city council to sanitize, the gum-stickers persevered and in 1999 the wall was declared a tourist attraction. Feel free to add your own well-chewed morsels to the Jackson Pollock–like display.

The New MarketFront

In a city as fast-moving as Seattle, not even a historical heirloom like Pike Place Market escapes a makeover. In 2015 ground was broken on the 'Pike Up' project, a 30,000-sq-ft extension of Pike Place. Made possible by the demolition of the Alaskan Way Viaduct, the MarketFront

Gum wall

complex opened in 2017 with new shops, restaurants and stalls, and links the market to the waterfront via terraces, staircases and green space.

Market History

Pike Place Market is the oldest continuously operating market in the nation. It was established in 1907 to give local farmers a place to sell their fruit and vegetables and bypass the middleman. Soon, the greengrocers made room for fishmongers, bakers, imported groceries, butchers, cheese sellers and purveyors of the rest of the Northwest's agricultural bounty. The market wasn't exactly architecturally robust – it's always been a thrown-together warren of sheds and stalls, haphazardly designed for utility – and was by no means an intentional tourist attraction. That came later.

An enthusiastic agricultural community spawned the market's heyday in the 1930s. Many of the first farmers were immigrants, a fact the market celebrates with annual themes acknowledging the contributions of various ethnic groups; past years have featured Japanese Americans, Italian Americans and Sephardic Jewish Americans.

By the 1960s, sales at the market were suffering from suburbanization, the growth of supermarkets and the move away from local, small-scale market gardening. Vast tracts of agricultural land were disappearing, replaced by such ventures as the Northgate Mall and Sea-Tac airport. The internment of Japanese American farmers during WWII had also taken its toll. The entire area became a bowery for the destitute and known as a center of ill repute.

The Market Today

In the wake of the 1962 World's Fair, plans were drawn up to bulldoze the market and build highrise office and apartment buildings on this piece of prime downtown real estate. Fortunately, public outcry prompted a voter's initiative to save the market. Subsequently, the space was cleaned up and restructured, and it has become once again the undeniable pulse of downtown: some 10 million people mill through the market each year. Thanks to the unique management of the market, social-services programs and low-income housing mix with commerce, and the market has maintained its gritty edge. These initiatives have prevented the area from ever sliding too far upmarket. A market law prohibits chain stores or franchises from setting up shop and ensures all businesses are locally owned. The one exception is, of course, Starbucks, which gets away with its market location because it is the coffee giant's first outlet.

Top Experiences 📷

Check Out Seattle Art Museum

While it doesn't have the size or star power of its contemporaries in New York and Chicago, the Seattle Art Museum (SAM) has a collection that feels uncommon, intimate and extraordinary. Its sterling selection of contemporary and antique art of the indigenous peoples of the Pacific Northwest alone makes this a required stop on any visit to the Emerald City.

◉ MAP P40, C5

📞 206-654-3210

www.seattleartmuseum.org

1300 1st Ave

adult/student
$24.95/14.95

🕐 10am-5pm Wed & Fri-Mon, to 9pm Thu

🚇 University St

Entrance Lobby

The museum's main building is guarded by a 48ft-high sculpture known as **Hammering Man** (by Jonathan Borofsky, 1991; pictured) and contains a cascading stairway inside guarded by Chinese statues called the *Art Ladder*. Look up to take in *Middle Fork* by John Grade, a giant plaster cast of an actual tree that hangs over the ticket desk. You'll get a good view of it from above as you take the escalator.

Modern & Contemporary Art

SAM has an enviable collection of modern art. Level 3 is home to Andy Warhol's *Double Elvis*, a silk-screen image of a young Presley firing a pistol right at the viewer, and Jackson Pollock's drippy (and trippy) *Sea Change*. The broad hallway at the top of the escalators has a small collection of exhibits from the Pilchuck Glass School, an excellent appetite whetter if you're heading over to Chihuly Garden & Glass (p70) later.

Native American Art

The Hauberg Gallery on level 3 is dedicated to the museum's impressive collections of art from the indigenous peoples of the Pacific Northwest coastal regions, including the Tlingit, Haida and Kwakwaka'wakw. Large wooden masks and colorful textiles are displayed thoughtfully here and the exhibits are accompanied by a video installation on contemporary Native American culture. There are also pieces from elsewhere in the Americas before European colonization, including a small room of artifacts from pre-Columbian Mesoamerica.

★ **Top Tips**

o Entry to the museum's permanent collections is free on the first Thursday of the month. Special exhibitions are half price.

o You can hear live jazz in the main entrance hall on the second Thursday of every month.

✕ **Take a Break**

SAM's excellent on-site restaurant **Taste** (☎206-903-5291; www.tastesam.com; mains $8-14; ⏰11am-5pm Wed, Fri, Sat & Sun, to 9pm Thu) is far more comprehensive and elegant than your average gallery cafe. Sometimes it even creatively fine-tunes its menu to tie in with the art exhibits on show.

Slip over to Heartwood Provisions (p44) for a heady art discussion over some happy hour craft cocktails.

Downtown, Pike Place & Waterfront

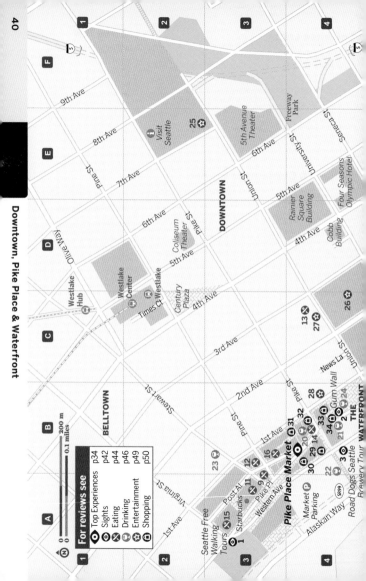

For reviews see

⊙ Top Experiences	p34
⊙ Sights	p42
✕ Eating	p44
🍷 Drinking	p46
✪ Entertainment	p49
🛍 Shopping	p50

BELLTOWN

DOWNTOWN

THE WATERFRONT

Pike Place Market

Seattle Free Walking Tours

Visit Seattle

Westlake Hub

Westlake Center

Times Sq Westlake

Century Plaza

Coliseum Theater

5th Avenue Theater

Freeway Park

Rainier Square Building

Cobb Building

Four Seasons Olympic Hotel

Gum Wall

Road Dogs Seattle Brewery Tour

Market Parking

Starbucks

Post Al

Pike Pl

Western Ave

Alaskan Way

9th Ave
8th Ave
7th Ave
6th Ave
5th Ave
4th Ave
3rd Ave
2nd Ave
1st Ave

Olive Way
Stewart St
Virginia St
Pine St
Pike St
Union St
University St
Seneca St
News La St
Union St

200 m
0.1 miles

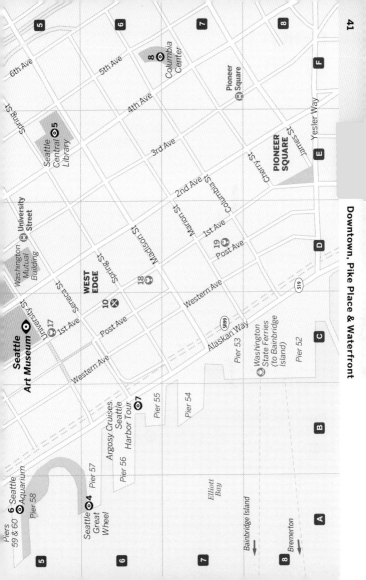

D5
6th Ave
Spring St

D6
5th Ave

8 Columbia Center

D7
4th Ave
3rd Ave
Pioneer Square

D8
2nd Ave
Yesler Way
F

Seattle Central Library 5
Spring St

PIONEER SQUARE
Cherry St
James St
E

Washington Mutual Building
University Street

2nd Ave
Columbia St
Marion St
1st Ave

WEST EDGE
Seneca St
Madison St
Spring St

18
19 Post Ave

Seattle Art Museum
University St
17
1st Ave
Post Ave
10
Western Ave

Western Ave
Alaskan Way
SR99
Pier 53

Washington State Ferries (to Bainbridge Island)
Pier 52
C

519
D

Argosy Cruises Seattle Harbor Tour 7
Pier 56
Pier 55
Pier 54

B

Piers 59 & 60 Seattle Aquarium
Pier 58
Pier 57

Seattle Great Wheel 4

Elliott Bay

Bainbridge Island

Bremerton

A

A5
A6
A7
A8

Sights

Seattle Free Walking Tours
WALKING

1 ⊙ MAP P40, A3

A nonprofit tour company that does an intimate two-hour walk takes in Pike Pl, the waterfront and Pioneer Sq, among other tours. Each tour is 'pay what you can,' and the company notes that comparable walking tours run around $20. Reserve online. (www.seattlefreewalkingtours.org; 2001 Western Ave; admission free)

Gum Wall
PUBLIC ART

2 ⊙ MAP P40, B4

Seattle's famous gum wall is one of those cultural monuments you can smell before you even see it. The sweet aroma of chewed gum wafts from this strip of Post Alley, which is completely covered in the stuff. It's a popular selfie spot, and is worth a peek for the sheer magnitude of it alone. It cannot be emphasized enough just how much gum there is! (Post Alley; ⊠University St)

Road Dogs Seattle Brewery Tour
TOURS

3 ⊙ MAP P40, B4

Road Dogs' popular three-hour Seattle Brewery tour takes in three breweries from a list of 25, from long-established microbreweries to nascent nano-businesses. To allow you to safely sup samples en route, you'll be picked up and whisked around in a minibus driven by a beer expert/driver.The company also runs local coffee and distillery tours. Book online. (📞206-249-9858; www.seattlebrewerytour.com; 1427 Western Ave; tours $79; ⊙10:30am, 2:30pm & 6pm Sun-Fri, 10:30am, 2:30pm & 6:30pm Fri & Sat)

Seattle Great Wheel
FERRIS WHEEL

4 ⊙ MAP P40, A6

This 175ft Ferris wheel was installed in June 2012 with 42 gondolas, each capable of carrying eight people on a 12-minute ride. The wheel sticks out over the water on Pier 57 and has quickly become synonymous with Seattle's ever-improving waterfront. It's the tallest of its type on the West Coast, though it pales in comparison with other behemoths such as the London Eye. (www.seattlegreatwheel.com; 1301 Alaskan Way; adult/child $14/9; ⊙10am-11pm Sun-Thu, to midnight Fri & Sat late Jun-early Sep, 11am-10pm Mon-Thu, to midnight Fri, 10am-midnight Sat, to 10pm Sun early Sep-late Jun; ⊠University St)

Seattle Central Library
LIBRARY

5 ⊙ MAP P40, E5

Rivaling the Space Needle and the Museum of Pop Culture for architectural ingenuity, Seattle Central Library looks like a giant diamond that's dropped in from outer space. Conceived by Rem Koolhaas and LMN Architects in 2004, the $165.5 million sculpture of glass and steel was designed to serve as a community gathering space, a tech center, a reading room and, of course, a massive storage facility for its one-million-plus books. Come here to enjoy art, architecture, coffee and literary comfort. (📞206-386-4636; www.spl.org; 1000 4th Ave; ⏰10am-8pm Mon-Thu, to 6pm Fri & Sat, noon-6pm Sun; 🅿; 🚇Pioneer Sq)

Seattle Aquarium   AQUARIUM

6 ◉ MAP P40, A5

Though not on a par with Seattle's nationally lauded Woodland Park Zoo, the aquarium – situated on Pier 59 in an attractive wooden building – is probably the most interesting sight on the waterfront, and it's a handy distraction for families with itchy-footed kids. (📞206-386-4300; www.seattleaquarium.org; 1483 Alaskan Way; adult/child $34.95/24.95; ⏰9:30am-5pm; 👪; 🚇University St)

Argosy Cruises Seattle Harbor Tour   CRUISE

7 ◉ MAP P40, B6

Argosy's popular Seattle Harbor Tour is a one-hour narrated excursion around Elliott Bay, the waterfront and the Port of Seattle. It departs from Pier 55. (📞206-623-1445; www.argosycruises.com; 1101 Alaskan Way, Pier 55; 1hr tour adult/child $31/17; 🚇University St)

Columbia Center   VIEWPOINT

8 ◉ MAP P40, F6

Everyone rushes tp the iconic Space Needle, but it's not the tallest Seattle viewpoint. That

Seattle Central Library

Downtown Seattle

Downtown Seattle, though impressive from a distance, is a bit of an anomaly. Instead of being the beating heart of the city, it's a fairly quiet, functional business district adjacent to Seattle's twin lures: Pike Place Market and Pioneer Sq.

What most people mean by 'downtown' is the collection of office buildings, hotels and retail shops between 2nd and 7th Aves. It's best to visit on a weekday, when throngs of people are working and shopping in the area. At night and on weekends it can feel rather desolate.

honor goes to the sleek, tinted-windowed Columbia Center at 932ft high with 76 floors. An elevator in the lobby takes you up to the free-access 40th floor, which has a Starbucks. From here you must take another elevator to the plush Sky View Observatory on the 73rd floor, from where you can look down on ferries, cars, islands, roofs and – ha ha – the Space Needle! (206-386-5564; www.skyviewobservatory.com; 701 5th Ave; adult/child $20/14; 10am-10pm late May-early Sep, to 8pm early Sep-late May; Pioneer Sq)

Eating

Beecher's Handmade Cheese   DELI $

Artisanal beer, artisanal coffee... next up, Seattle brings you artisanal cheese and it's made as you watch in this always-crowded Pike Place nook, where you can buy all kinds of cheese-related paraphernalia.

As for that long, snaking, almost permanent queue – that's people lining up for the wonderful home-made mac 'n' cheese that comes in two different-sized tubs and is simply divine. (206-956-1964; www.beechershandmadecheese.com; 1600 Pike Pl; snacks $5-12; 9am-6pm; Westlake)

Heartwood Provisions   FUSION $$$

10   MAP P40, C6

Cocktails are having a moment as the alcoholic libation du jour in Seattle and nowhere is that more clear than at Heartwood, a handsome restaurant and bar with a menu of mixed drinks that is unmatched. Come for dinner, where each dish is infused with Southeast Asian flavors and has its own cocktail pairing (optional for an additional $7). (206-582-3505; www.heartwoodsea.com; 1103 1st Ave; mains $24-37; 4:30-10pm Sun-Thu, to 11pm Fri & Sat, also 9:30am-2pm Sat & Sun; University St)

Piroshky Piroshky BAKERY $

11 ✖ MAP P40, A3

Piroshky knocks out its delectable sweet and savory Russian pies and pastries in a space about the size of a walk-in closet. Get the savory smoked salmon pâté or the sauerkraut with onion, and follow it up with the chocolate-cream hazelnut roll or a fresh rhubarb piroshki. (📞206-441-6068; www.piroshkybakery.com; 1908 Pike Pl; snacks $3-6; ⊙8am-7pm Mon-Fri, to 7:30pm Sat & Sun; ⊠Westlake)

Café Campagne FRENCH $$

12 ✖ MAP P40, B3

Short of teleporting over to Paris, this is about as Gallic as a Seattleite can get. Inside Café Campagne's effortlessly elegant interior you can live vicariously as a French poseur over steamed mussels, hanger steaks, generous portions of *frites* and crispy vegetables. Save room for the crème brûlée dessert. Should you be sufficiently satisfied, consider coming back for weekend brunch. (📞206-728-2233; www.cafecampagne.com; 1600 Post Alley; mains $18-28; ⊙10am-10pm Mon-Fri, from 8am Sat & Sun; ⊠Westlake)

Wild Ginger ASIAN $$$

13 ✖ MAP P40, C4

A tour of the Pacific Rim – via China, Indonesia, Malaysia, Vietnam and Seattle, of course – is the wide-ranging theme at this highly popular downtown fusion restaurant. The signature fragrant duck goes down nicely with a glass of Riesling. The restaurant also provides food for the swanky Triple Door (p49) dinner club downstairs. (📞206-623-4450; www.wildginger.net; 1401 3rd Ave; mains $19-34; ⊙11:30am-10pm Mon-Thu, to 11pm Fri & Sat, 4-9pm Sun; ⊠University St)

Matt's in the Market NORTHWESTERN US $$$

14 ✖ MAP P40, B4

Matt's, run by a former Pike Place Market fish-thrower, is perched above the bustle of the market with views out over the famous clock. Most of the ingredients on the menu come from down below. Expect plenty of fish, fresh veg and organic meats. (📞206-467-7909; www.mattsinthemarket.com; 94 Pike St; mains lunch $15-21, dinner $38-48; ⊙11:30am-2:30pm & 5:30-10pm Mon-Sat; ⊠Westlake)

Pink Door Ristorante ITALIAN $$$

15 ✖ MAP P40, A3

A restaurant like no other, the Pink Door is probably the only place in the US (the world?) where you can enjoy fabulous *linguine alle vongole* (pasta with clams and pancetta) and other Italian favorites while watching live jazz, burlesque cabaret or – we kid you not – a trapeze artist swinging from the 20ft ceiling. (📞206-443-3241; www.thepinkdoor.net; 1919 Post Alley; mains $19-30; ⊙11:30am-10pm Mon-Thu, to 11pm Fri & Sat, 4-10pm Sun; ⊠Westlake)

Drinking

Arty Navigation

Look down! Seattle's public art extends to its hatch covers (manholes). Nineteen of them have been emblazoned with an imprint of a downtown map with your location marked. It's impossible to get lost.

Pike Place Chowder

SEAFOOD $

16 MAP P40, B3

Proof that some of the best culinary ideas are almost ridiculously simple, this Pike Place Market hole-in-the-wall takes that New England favorite (clam chowder) and gives it a dynamic West Coast makeover. You can choose from four traditional chowders in four different sizes accompanied by four different salads. Then you can fight to eat it at one of four tables. (📞206-267-2537; www.pikeplacechowder.com; 1530 Post Alley; medium chowder $8.75; ⏱11am-5pm; 🚇Westlake)

Drinking

Ancient Grounds

CAFE

17 MAP P40, C5

If it's not enough that this cozy coffee nook serves some of the best espresso shots in the city, Ancient Grounds also doubles as a showroom for a well-curated selection of antiques. While waiting for your latte, you can pick through a rack of vintage kimonos or peruse

a display of wooden masks from indigenous communities of the Pacific Northwest. (📞206-7749-0747; 1220 1st Ave; ⏱7:30am-4:30pm Mon-Fri, noon-6pm Sat; 🚇University St)

Bookstore Bar

BAR

18 MAP P40, D6

Cementing downtown's reputation as a fount of good hotel bars is the Bookstore (encased in the front window of the Alexis Hotel), which mixes books stacked on handsome wooden shelves with whiskey – an excellent combination (ask Dylan Thomas). There are over 100 varieties of Scotch and bourbon available, plus the full gamut of weighty literary tomes from Melville to Twain. (📞206-624-4844; www.alexishotel.com; 1007 1st Ave; ⏱7am-11pm Mon-Fri, from 8am Sat, 8am-10pm Sun; 🚇Pioneer Sq)

Owl & Thistle

IRISH PUB

19 MAP P40, D7

One of the best Irish pubs in the city, the dark, multiroomed Owl & Thistle is located slap-bang downtown but misses most of the tourist traffic because it's hidden in Post Ave. (📞206-621-7777; www.owlnthistle.com; 808 Post Ave; ⏱11am-2am; 🚇Pioneer Sq)

Radiator Whiskey

WHISKEY BAR

20 🚇 MAP P40, B4

A fruitful marriage of style and substance, Radiator Whiskey, on the top floor of Pike Place Market (p34), has exactly the amount of rustic design you'd want from a whiskey bar that has dozens of bourbons, ryes and single malts on offer. There are other spirits too, as well as a drink list that includes four takes on the classic Manhattan. (📞206-467-4268; www.radiatorwhiskey.com; 94 Pike St; ⏱4pm-midnight Mon-Sat; 🚇University St)

Storyville Coffee CAFE

There are so many coffee bars in Seattle that it's sometimes hard to see the forest for the trees, unless it's the kind of wood that adorns the curved bar of Storyville (see 14 ⊗ MAP P40, B4). Welcome to one of Seattle's newer luxury coffee chains, whose two downtown locations (the other one is at 1st and Madison) attract a mixture of tourists and locals looking for excellent coffee. (📞206-780-5777; www.storyville.com; 94 Pike St; ⏱6:59am-6pm; 📶; 🚇Westlake)

Alibi Room BAR

21 🔘 MAP P40, B4

Hidden down Post Alley opposite the beautifully disgusting 'gum wall' (p36), the Alibi feels like an old speakeasy or perhaps the perfect place to hide from the perfect crime (or all the Pike Place crowds). Dark and cavernous, it provides surprisingly good entertainment with regular DJ nights, art installations, stand-up performances and experimental-film screenings.

If you're peckish it has a menu of pretty damn good pizza ($19 to

The not-quite-original Starbucks store (p48)

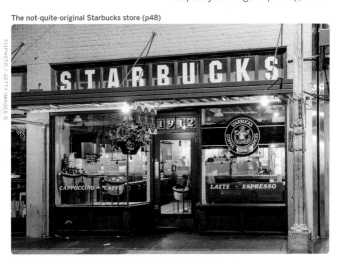

Downtown, Pike Place & Waterfront Drinking

Starbucks – It Started Here (Almost)

It's practically impossible to walk through the door of **Starbucks** (Map p40, A3; ☎206-448-8762; www.1912pike.com; 1912 Pike Pl; ⊘6am-9pm; ◙Westlake) in Pike Place Market without appearing in someone's Facebook photo, so dense is the tourist traffic. But, while this hallowed business might be the world's oldest surviving Starbucks store, it is not – as many assume – the world's first Starbucks location, nor is it Seattle's oldest espresso bar.

The original Starbucks opened in 1971 at 2000 Western Ave (at Western Ave's north end). It moved to its current location, a block away, in 1976. The honor of Seattle's oldest continuously running coffee bar goes to Café Allegro (p121) in the U District, which opened in 1975.

Until the early 1980s Starbucks operated purely as a retail store that sold coffee beans and equipment (plus the odd taster cup). The company didn't open up its first espresso bar until 1984, after CEO Howard Shultz returned from an epiphanic trip to Italy. The Pike Place cafe is unique in that, in keeping with the traditional unbranded ethos of the market, it doesn't sell food or baked goods – just coffee.

$23) and other snacky bar foods. (☎206-623-3180; www.seattlealibi.com; 85 Pike Pl; ⊘11:30am-2am, food to 1am; ◙University St)

Zig Zag Café
COCKTAIL BAR

22 MAP P40, B4

If you're writing a research project on Seattle's culinary history, you'll need to reserve a chapter for Zig Zag Café. This is the bar that repopularized gin-based Jazz Age cocktail 'The Last Word' in the early 2000s. The drink went viral and the Zig Zag's nattily attired mixers were rightly hailed as the city's finest alchemists. (☎206-625-1146; www.zigzagseattle.com; 1501 Western Ave; ⊘5pm-2am; ◙University St)

Nest
ROOFTOP BAR

23 ◙ MAP P40, B3

Like many rooftop bars in major US cities, the Nest is overpriced and usually crowded with cliques of lawyers and PR executives. But the views of the downtown skyline rolling out along the Puget Sound with Mt Rainier visible in the distance on clear evenings make it well worth at least one drink. (☎206-512-1096; 110 Stewart St; ⊘5pm-midnight Sun-Thu, from 3pm Fri & Sat)

Pike Pub & Brewery
BREWERY

24 ◙ MAP P40, B4

Leading the way in the US micro-brewery revolution, this brewpub was an early starter, opening in 1989 underneath Pike Place Market. Today it continues to serve good pub food (mains $15 to $26) and hop-heavy, made-on-site beers in a busily decorated but fun multilevel space. Free tours of the brewery are available. (☎206-622-6044; www.pikebrewing.com; 1415 1st Ave; ⏱11am-midnight Sun-Thu, to 1am Fri & Sat; 🚇University St)

Entertainment

A Contemporary Theatre
THEATER

25 ⭐ MAP P40, E2

One of the three big theater companies in the city, the ACT fills its $30 million home at Kreielsheimer Place with performances by Seattle's best thespians and occasional big-name actors. Terraced seating surrounds a central stage and the interior has gorgeous architectural embellishments. (ACT; ☎206-292-7676; www.acttheatre.org; 700 Union St; 🚇University St)

Benaroya Concert Hall
CONCERT HALL

26 ⭐ MAP P40, C4

With a bill of almost $120 million in construction costs, it's no wonder the Benaroya Concert Hall, the primary venue of the **Seattle Symphony**, oozes luxury. The minute you step into the glass-enclosed lobby of the performance hall, you're overwhelmed by views of Elliott Bay; on clear days you might even see the snowy peaks of the Olympic Range in the distance. (☎206-215-4747; www.seattlesymphony.org/benaroyahall; 200 University St; 🚇University St)

Triple Door
LIVE PERFORMANCE

27 ⭐ MAP P40, C4

This club downstairs from the Wild Ginger (p45) restaurant is a Seattle mainstay with a liberal booking policy that includes country and rock as well as jazz, gospel, R&B, world music and burlesque performances. There's a full menu and a smaller lounge upstairs, called the **Musicquarium**, with an aquarium and free live music. (☎206-838-4333; www.thetripledoor.net; 216 Union St; 🚇University St)

Showbox
LIVE MUSIC

28 ⭐ MAP P40, B4

This cavernous 1137-capacity showroom – which hosts mostly national touring acts, ranging from indie rock to hip-hop – reinvents itself every few years and successfully rode the grunge bandwagon while it lasted. It first opened in 1939 and its dressing-room walls could probably tell some stories – everyone from Duke Ellington to Ice Cube has played here. (☎206-628-3151; www.showboxpresents.com; 1426 1st Ave; 🚇University St)

Shopping

Old Seattle Paperworks

POSTERS, MAGAZINES

29 MAP P40, B4

If you like decorating your home with old magazine covers from *Life, Time* and *Rolling Stone*, or have a penchant for art deco tourist posters from the 1930s, or are looking for that rare Hendrix concert flyer from 1969, this is your nirvana. It's in Pike Place Market's Down Under section. (206-623-2870; 1501 Pike Pl; 10am-5pm; Westlake)

Market Magic

MAGIC

30 MAP P40, B4

Selling fake dog poop, stink bombs, water-squirting rings and magic tricks, this Pike Place Market (p34) magic shop is heaven for aspiring magicians, pranksters, school kids, and grown-ups who wish they were still school kids. (206-624-4271; www.marketmagicshop.com; 1501 Pike Pl; 10am-5pm Mon-Sat, from 10:30am Sun; Westlake)

Metsker Maps

MAPS

31 MAP P40, B4

In its high-profile location on 1st Ave, this 65-year-old map shop sells all kinds of useful things for the traveler, from maps and guidebooks to various accessories. It also has a good selection of armchair-travel lit and pretty spinning globes for the dreamers. (206-623-8747; www.metskers.com; 1511 1st Ave; 9am-8pm Mon-

Bainbridge Island

ANDRIANA SYVANYCH / SHUTTERSTOCK

Bainbridge Island

Tap the average Seattleite about their most cherished weekend excursion and they could surprise you with a dark horse – a cheap and simple ride (tickets from $8.50) on the commuter ferry across Puget Sound to Bainbridge Island. There's nothing quite like being surrounded by water and seeing Seattle's famous skyline disappearing in the ferry's foamy wake.

The ride is only 35 minutes each way and is free coming back from the island. Catch the ferry at Pier 52 on the waterfront.

Fri, from 10am Sat, 10am-6pm Sun; 🚊Westlake)

Left Bank Books
BOOKS

32 🔒 MAP P40, B4

This collective of more than 40 years displays zines in *español*, revolutionary pamphlets, essays by Chomsky and an inherent suspicion of authority. You're in Seattle, just in case you forgot. (📞206-662-0195; www.leftbankbooks.com; 92 Pike St; ⏰10am-7pm Mon-Sat, 11am-6pm Sun; 🚊Westlake)

DeLaurenti's
FOOD

33 🔒 MAP P40, B4

A Pike Place Market veteran, this Italian grocery store/deli has been run by the same family since 1946. Not needing to roll with the times, it offers a beautifully old-fashioned selection of wine, cheese, sausages, hams and pasta, along with a large range of capers, olive oils and anchovies. The sandwich counter is a great place to order panini, salads and pizza. (📞206-622-0141; www.delaurenti.com; 1435 1st Ave; snacks $5-12; ⏰9am-6pm Mon-Sat, 10am-5pm Sun; 🚊University St)

Tenzing Momo
GIFTS & SOUVENIRS

34 🔒 MAP P40, B4

Doing a good impersonation of one of the magic shops in Diagon Alley from the *Harry Potter* books, Tenzing Momo is an old-school natural apothecary with shelves of mysterious glass bottles filled with herbs and tinctures to treat any ailment. It's in Pike Place Market's Economy Market Building. (📞206-338-0193; www.tenzingmomo.com; 93 Pike St; ⏰10am-6pm Mon-Sat, to 5pm Sun; 🚊University St)

Explore

Pioneer Square, International District & SoDo

Seattle's birthplace retains its 'Skid Row' roots with redbrick architecture and rambunctious street life. The legacy of the International District (ID) as home to many of the city's Southeast Asian immigrant communities makes for unique shopping and exquisite dining, while SoDo is a warehouse district attracting new distilleries and dispensaries.

The Short List

○ **Klondike Gold Rush National Historical Park (p58)** *Reliving the spirit of the gold rush at this inspiring museum.*

○ **Jade Garden (p62)** *Satisfying lunchtime Asian food cravings at this boisterous dim sum restaurant in the International District.*

○ **CenturyLink Field (p64)** *Warming up in the bars of Pioneer Square before attending a football or soccer game.*

Getting There & Around

🚌 There's no shortage of bus service here.

🚈 Central Link light-rail from Sea-Tac Airport stops at Pioneer Square station or International District/Chinatown station.

🚋 The First Hill Streetcar runs from S Jackson St in Pioneer Square through the ID, Central District (CD) and First Hill to Capitol Hill.

Neighborhood Map on p56

Totem in Pioneer Square Park ARTYOORAN / SHUTTERSTOCK ©

Top Experiences 📷

Glimpse the Past at Pioneer Square

Many important architectural heirlooms are concentrated in Pioneer Square, the district that sprang up in the wake of the 1889 Great Fire. Instantly recognizable by its handsome redbrick buildings, the neighborhood showcases the Richardsonian Romanesque architectural style, strongly influenced by America's Chicago School.

◎ MAP P56, C2

btwn Alaskan Way S, S King St, 5th Ave S, 2nd Ave ext & Columbia St

🚋 First Hill Streetcar

Grand Central Arcade

The lovely **Grand Central Arcade** (Map p56, C3; 📞206-623-7417; 214 1st Ave S; 🚋First Hill Streetcar) was originally Squire's Opera House, erected in 1879. When the Opera House was destroyed in the Great Fire, it was rebuilt as the Squire-Latimer Building in 1890 and later became the Grand Central Hotel. The hotel closed during the Depression, but it underwent a major restoration in the 1970s and now contains two floors of shops.

Pioneer Building

Built in 1891, the magnificent **Pioneer Building** (Map p56, C2; 606 1st Ave S; 🚋First Hill Streetcar) facing Pioneer Square Park is one of the finest Victorian buildings in Seattle and features many of the classic components of Richardsonian Romanesque; look for the Roman arches, a recessed main doorway, curvaceous bay windows and decorative flourishes, most notably the two frontal columns that frame some skillfully embellished bricks.

Smith Tower

A mere dwarf amid Seattle's impressive modern stash of skyscrapers, the 42-story neoclassical **Smith Tower** (pictured; Map p56, D2; 📞206-622-4004; www.smithtower.com; 506 2nd Ave; adult/child $20/16; ⏰10am-11pm Sun-Wed, to midnight Thu-Sat; 🚋Pioneer Sq) was, for half a century after its construction in 1914, the tallest building west of Chicago. The beaux arts–inspired lobby is paneled in onyx and marble, and the brass-and-copper elevator is still manually operated by a uniformed attendant. You can visit the observation deck at the 35th-floor Observatory (formerly called the Chinese Room), which has an ornate wooden ceiling.

★ **Top Tips**

o Choose a fine day and you can soak up the atmosphere of Pioneer Square while sitting in the once gritty, but now pretty, Occidental Park (p60).

o To get the full lowdown on the buildings you'll need to get underneath them – Bill Speidel's Underground Tour (p58) can help.

o There's a handy information kiosk giving out neighborhood maps in Occidental Park.

✕ **Take a Break**

For coffee and some rather good almond croissants, tune into the neighborhood zeitgeist at Zeitgeist Coffee (p62).

If you're feeling peckish, raid the deli counter at slavishly sustainable London Plane (p60).

A
- Pier 53
- Washington State Ferries (to Bainbridge Island)
- Pier 52
- THE WATERFRONT
- Elliott Bay
- Pier 50
- Water Taxis
- Pier 48

B
- Columbia St
- Post Ave
- Western Ave
- Alaskan Way
- SR99
- 16
- S Washington St
- Grand Central Arcade
- S Main St
- Nord Al
- Occidental Square
- S Jackson St
- Occidental Mall
- S King St
- Alaskan Way S
- SR99
- S Railroad Way

C
- 1st Ave
- Cherry St
- 14 Pioneer Square
- James St
- Bill Speidel's Underground Tour
- 3 Pioneer Building
- Pioneer Square Architecture
- Yesler Way
- 10
- 19
- 7
- Occidental Park
- Klondike Gold Rush National Historical Park
- 9
- 1
- Occidental Ave S
- 12
- 17 S
- 2nd Ave S
- 1st Ave S
- Occidental Ave S
- P
- PIONEER SQUARE
- 20
- 2 22 24
- 21

D
- 2nd Ave
- 3rd Ave
- Smith Tower
- 2nd Ave Ext S

For reviews see
- ◉ Top Experiences   p54
- ◉ Sights   p58
- ⊗ Eating   p60
- 🍷 Drinking   p62
- ★ Entertainment   p64
- 🔒 Shopping   p64

0 ————————— 200 m
0 ————————— 0.1 miles

Pioneer Square, International District & SoDo

E **F** **G** **H**

Harborview Park

FIRST HILL

Jefferson St
5th Ave
6th Ave

PIONEER SQUARE

Terrace St

Yesler Way

Prefontaine Pl S
3rd Ave S
4th Ave S
5th Ave S
6th Ave S

S Washington St

JAPANTOWN

Kobe Terrace Park

S Main St ⊗18
⊗8

5th & Jackson/ Japantown

7th & Jackson/ Chinatown
11 ⊗▶
13 ⊗▶

Maynard Ave S
7th Ave S
Canton Al S
8th Ave S

S Jackson St

King Street Station
5 ⊙

Union Station

International District/ Chinatown

CHINATOWN

⊗15

⊙6

Cantrail

King St Station (Amtrak)

S King St
25

Seattle Pinball Museum 4

Maynard Al S

Wing Luke Museum of the Asian Pacific American Experience

INTERNATIONAL DISTRICT

S Weller St

4th Ave S
5th Ave S
6th Ave S

23

S Lane St

Maynard Ave S
7th Ave S
8th Ave S

S Dearborn St

Airport Way S

90

S Charles St

E **F** **G** **H**

Sights

Klondike Gold Rush National Historical Park

MUSEUM

1 MAP P56, D3

Run by the US National Park Service, this wonderful museum has exhibits, photos and news clippings from the 1897 Klondike gold rush, when a Seattle-on-steroids acted as a fueling depot for prospectors bound for the Yukon in Canada. Free entry! (206-553-3000; www.nps.gov/klse; 319 2nd Ave S; admission free; 9am-5pm Jun-Aug, 10am-5pm Tue-Sun Sep-Feb, 10am-5pm Mar-May; First Hill Streetcar)

Klondike Gold Rush National Historical Park

BRIAN LOGAN PHOTOGRAPHY / SHUTTERSTOCK ©

Westland Distillery

DISTILLERY

2 MAP P56, C6

On a drizzly day in Puget Sound, the damp essence of Seattle isn't a million miles from the Western Isles of Scotland, a comparison not lost on the whiskey-makers of Westland, one of Seattle's finest distilleries. From its plush tasting room and factory in SoDo, this company serves already legendary micro-distilled single malt. (206-767-7250; www.westlanddistillery.com; 2931 1st Ave S; tour $17.34; noon-7pm Tue-Thu, 11am-8pm Fri & Sat, noon-6pm Sun, tours noon-4pm Wed-Sat; 50)

Bill Speidel's Underground Tour

WALKING

3 MAP P56, C2

This cleverly conceived tour of Seattle's historic 'underground' – the part of the city that got buried by landfill in the 1890s – benefits from its guides, who are excellent, using wit and animation to relate Seattle's unusual early history. (206-682-4646; www.undergroundtour.com; 608 1st Ave; adult/senior/child $22/20/10; departs every hour 10am-6pm Oct-Mar, 9am-7pm Apr-Sep; Pioneer Sq)

Seattle Pinball Museum

MUSEUM

4 MAP P56, G4

Got kids? Got kid-like tendencies? Love the buzzers and bells of good old-fashioned analog machines? Lay aside your iPad apps and become a pinball wizard for the day in this fantastic games room in the International District, with machines from 1960s retro to futuristic. Admission buys you unlimited games for the day. (📞206-623-0759; www.seattlepinballmuseum.com; 508 Maynard Ave S; adult/child $15/12; ⏱noon-6pm Sun, Mon & Thu, to 8pm Fri & Sat; 👬; 🚊First Hill Streetcar)

King Street Station LANDMARK

5 ⊙ MAP P56, E4

One of the pillars on which Seattle built its early fortunes, the old Great Northern Railroad depot, was given a much-needed face-lift in the early 2010s after decades of neglect. Serving as the western terminus of the famous Empire Builder train that runs cross-country between Seattle and Chicago, the station

building was designed to imitate St Mark's bell tower in Venice. (303 S Jackson St; 🚊International District/Chinatown)

Wing Luke Museum of the Asian Pacific American Experience MUSEUM

6 ⊙ MAP P56, H4

The beautiful Wing Luke museum examines Asia Pacific American culture, focusing on prickly issues such as Chinese settlement in the 1880s and Japanese internment camps during WWII. There are also art exhibits and a preserved immigrant apartment. Guided tours are available; the first Thursday of the month is free (with extended hours until 8pm). (📞206-623-5124; www.wingluke.

King Street Station

PLUME PHOTOGRAPHY / SHUTTERSTOCK ©

Richardsonian Romanesque

Pioneer Square's hallmark architecture is a revivalist style named after American architect Henry Richardson from Louisiana, who first popularized it in Boston and Chicago in the 1870s and '80s. It harks back to the medieval European genre of Romanesque, in vogue from the 10th to the 12th centuries. Features of Richardsonian Romanesque include classic Roman arches, heavy, rough-cut masonry, recessed doorways and the use of decorative columns and bricks.

org; 719 S King St; adult/child $17/12; ⏰10am-5pm Tue-Sun; 🚋First Hill Streetcar)

Occidental Park   PARK

7 MAP P56, C3

Once a rather rough-and-tumble place, Occidental Park has undergone a renaissance thanks largely to a partnership between the City of Seattle and a couple of nonprofit groups. Following an urban-renewal campaign in 2015, the park has been outfitted with attractive seating, outdoor games (including chess and table football), licensed buskers and a regular posse of food carts. (📞206-684-4075; 117 S Washington St; ⏰6am-10pm; 🚋First Hill Streetcar)

Eating

Maneki   JAPANESE $$

8 🍴 MAP P56, G3

For an unforgettable dining experience, make a reservation for one of Maneki's tatami mat dining rooms (paper and wood lattice private chambers with seating on the floor) and feast on a meal of traditional Japanese cuisine and sake. The fish here is legendarily fresh and the bar (open until midnight) is full of friendly conversation. (📞206-622-2631; www.manekirestaurant.com; 304 6th Ave S; mains $14-26; ⏰5:30-10:30pm Tue-Sun; 🚋First Hill Streetcar)

London Plane   CAFE, DELI $$

9 🍴 MAP P56, D3

Matt Dillon (the Seattle chef, not the Hollywood actor) moved less than a block from his now-closed Bar Sajor to open London Plane, a hybrid cafe, flower shop, deli and breakfast spot that maintains the French country kitchen feel that has become Dillon's trademark. (📞206-624-1374; www.thelondonplaneseattle.com; 300 Occidental Ave S; small plates $7-19; ⏰8am-6pm Mon-Fri, from 9am Sat, 9am-3pm Sun; 🚋First Hill Streetcar)

Nirmal's   INDIAN $$

10 🍴 MAP P56, D2

In a short period of time Nirmal's has established itself as Seattle's premier Indian fine-dining experience. The menu is a good balance of recognizable curry and tandoori dishes, as well as treats only familiar to those who have been to the subcontinent and exciting fusion plates that nod to its Pacific Northwest locale (we're looking at you Dungeness crab curry). (206-388-2196; www.nirmalseattle.com; 106 Occidental Ave S; mains $17-27; 11am-2pm & 5:30-10pm Mon-Fri, 5:30-10pm Sat; Pioneer Sq)

Seven Stars Pepper   SICHUAN $$

11 MAP P56, H3

Don't be put off by Seven Stars Pepper's location on the 2nd floor of a run-down strip mall: this Szechuan restaurant is one of the best in the city. Everything on the menu is exceptional, but the hand-cut *dan dan* noodles are a must-order. They are thick and flavorful with the just the right amount of chewiness. (206-568-6446; www.sevenstarspepper.com; 1207 S Jackson St; mains $9-20; 11am-3pm & 5-9:30pm Mon-Wed, 11am-9:30pm Thu, to 10pm Fri & Sat, to 9pm Sun; First Hill Streetcar)

Salumi Artisan Cured Meats   SANDWICHES $

12 MAP P56, D4

This well-loved deli used to be known for the long lines at its tiny storefront, and although they've moved to a bigger spot, you can still expect a wait for the legendary Italian-quality salami and cured-meat sandwiches (grilled lamb, pork shoulder, meatballs). You can expect a regular sandwich menu, as well as daily sandwich, soup and pasta specials. (206-621-8772; www.salumicuredmeats.com; 404 Occidental Ave S; sandwiches $10.50-12.50; 11am-3pm Mon-Sat; International District/Chinatown)

Tamarind Tree   VIETNAMESE $

13 MAP P56, H3

Serving upscale food at entry-level prices in a massively popular dining room, this legendary place has a nuanced menu that includes everything from satays and salad rolls to *pho* and rice cakes (squid-, prawn- and pork-filled fried crepes). Tamarind Tree donates some of its profits to the

Occidental Park

TS PHOTOGRAPHER / SHUTTERSTOCK ©

Make a Real Change

Pioneer Square's large population of unhoused people may give some visitors pause, but it's important to keep in mind that they are citizens of the neighborhood the same as anyone else, and pose no more of a threat than their housed neighbors. Other than helping out with spare change, one way to give is buying the weekly newspaper *Real Change*. You'll see vendors, many of them unhoused people, selling it on the street for $2 (vendors buy the paper for $0.60 a copy and keep the profit). The paper, founded in 1994, generates nearly $1 million a year for homelessness causes.

Vietnam Scholarship Foundation. It's hidden at the back of an ugly car park. (206-860-1414; www.tamarindtreerestaurant.com; 1036 S Jackson St; mains $10-13; 10am-10pm Sun-Thu, to 11pm Fri & Sat; First Hill Streetcar)

Biscuit Bitch   SOUTHERN US $

14 MAP P56, D1

Biscuit Bitch proudly bills itself as trailer-park cuisine, which will only be off-putting to those who haven't experienced the nirvana of tucking into an order of thick, crumbly biscuits and rich gravy. This is one location of a small local chain. Things are always busy, but the line moves fast and the staff are a blast. (206-623-1859; https://biscuitbitch.com; 621 3rd Ave; mains $7-10; 7am-2pm Mon-Fri, 8am-3pm Sat & Sun; Pioneer Sq)

Jade Garden   CHINESE $

15 MAP P56, H4

Usually mentioned near the top of the list of best places for dim

sum in the ID, Jade Garden offers a good range of delicacies with everything from standard, newbie-friendly shrimp dumplings and steamed pork buns to more exotic plates such as black cylinders of sesame-paste gel and, of course, chicken feet. (206-622-8181; 424 7th Ave S; dim sum $2-4, mains $8-13; 10am-2:30am Mon-Sat, to 1am Sun; First Hill Streetcar)

Drinking

Saké Nomi   SAKE

16 MAP P56, B2

Whether you're a sake connoisseur or a casual enjoyer, you're likely to expand your palate and your cultural horizons at this cozy retailer and tasting room in Pioneer Square. The Japanese and American wife-husband duo who run the place have a clear love for what they do, which shows in their wonderfully educational tasting menu. (206-467-7253; www.sakenomi.us; 76 S Washington St; flight of 3 $22; 2-

10pm Tue, Wed, Fri & Sat, from 5pm Thu,
2-6pm Sun; 🚇First Hill Streetcar)

Zeitgeist Coffee CAFE

17 📍 MAP P56, D4

Possibly Seattle's best (and busiest) indie coffee bar, Zeitgeist brews smooth *doppio macchiatos* to go with its sweet almond croissants and other luscious baked goods. The atmosphere is trendy industrial, with brick walls and large windows for people-watching. Soups, salads and sandwiches are also on offer. (📞206-583-0497; www.zeitgeistcoffee.com; 171 S Jackson St; ⏰6am-7pm Mon-Fri, from 7am Sat, 8am-6pm Sun; 📶; 🚇First Hill Streetcar)

Panama Hotel
Tea & Coffee House CAFE

18 📍 MAP P56, G3

The intensely atmospheric tea-house inside the Panama Hotel has such a thoroughly back-in-time feel that you'll be reluctant to pull out your laptop (although there is wi-fi). It's in a 1910, National Treasure–designated building containing the only remaining Japanese bath-house in the US, and doubles as a memorial to the neighborhood's Japanese residents forced into internment camps during WWII. (📞206-515-4000; www.panamahotel.net; 607 S Main St; tea $3-6; ⏰8am-9pm; 📶; 🚇First Hill Streetcar)

Biscuit Bitch

Fuel
SPORTS BAR

19 🚻 MAP P56, D2

This TV-filled sports bar is the favored spot in Pioneer Square for Mariners and Seahawks fans on game day. Tuck your elbows in and inhale deeply as you enter. (☎206-405-3835; www.fuelseattle.com; 164 S Washington St; ⏱3-10pm Mon, to midnight Tue & Thu, to 2am Wed, 11:30am-2am Fri & Sat, to 10pm Sun; 🚇Pioneer Sq)

Entertainment

CenturyLink Field
STADIUM

20 ⭐ MAP P56, D6

The late, mostly unlamented King-dome, long Seattle's biggest eye-sore, was once the home field for the city's professional baseball and football franchises. Then it was imploded spectacularly in 2000 and replaced by this 72,000-seat stadium, home of the NFL **Seattle Seahawks** (www.seahawks.com) and Seattle's soccer team the **Sounders** (www.seattlesounders. net). (www.centurylinkfield.com; 800 Occidental Ave S; 🚇Stadium)

T-Mobile Park
STADIUM

21 ⭐ MAP P56, C6

Home of Seattle's pro baseball team, the **Mariners** (www.mariners. org), the $517 million T-Mobile Park (originally Safeco Field) opened in July 1999. With its retractable roof, 47,000 seats and real grass, the stadium was funded by taxpay-ers and tourists with the Mariners

coughing up the difference. The stadium's unique design means it commands fantastic views of the surrounding mountains and Puget Sound. (☎206-346-4241; www.mlb. com/mariners/ballpark; 1250 1st Ave S; 1¼hr tours adult/child $12/10; ⏱ tours 10:30am, 12:30pm & 2:30pm non-game days Apr-Oct; 🚇Stadium)

Shopping

Filson
SPORTS & OUTDOORS

22 🔒 MAP P56, C6

Founded in 1897 as the original outfitters for prospectors head-ing for the Klondike, Filson is a long-standing Seattle legend that, in 2015, opened up this hugely impressive flagship store in SoDo. Wall-mounted bison heads and sepia-toned photos evoke the Klondike spirit, while flop-down so-fas and literary tomes encourage lingering. (☎206-622-3147; www.fil son.com; 1741 1st Ave S; ⏱10am-6pm Mon-Sat, noon-5pm Sun; 🚇Stadium)

Uwajimaya
MALL

23 🔒 MAP P56, F5

Founded by Fujimatsu Moriguchi, one of the few Japanese Ameri-cans to return here from the WWII internment camps, this large department and grocery store is a cornerstone of Seattle's Asian community. It has everything from fresh fish and exotic fruits and vegetables to cooking utensils and homegoods. It's a terrific place to go gift shopping. (☎206-624-6248; www.uwajimaya.com; 600 5th Ave S;

First Thursday Art Walk

Art walks are two a penny in US cities these days, but they were pretty much an unknown quantity when the pioneering artists of Pioneer Square instituted their first amble around the local galleries in 1981. Aside from gluing together Pioneer Square's network of 50-plus galleries, the **art walk** (☎206-667-0687; www.firstthursdayseattle. com; Occidental Park; ⏱hours vary by venue) is a good excuse to admire creative public sculpture, sip decent coffee (many cafes serve as de-facto galleries), browse an array of stalls set up in Occidental Park (p60), and get to know the neighborhood and its people.

The Art Walk is self-guided, but you can pick up a map from the information booth in Occidental Park. Free parking is also offered from 5pm to 10pm.

⏱8am-10pm Mon-Sat, 9am-9pm Sun; 🚋First Hill Streetcar)

Ganja Goddess

DISPENSARY

24 🔒 MAP P56, C6

Ganja Goddess is a popular weed dispensary known for its helpful and unpretentious staff and free shuttle service picking and dropping off clients in and around Seattle's downtown core. It has a great selection and takes debit and credit cards. (☎206-682-7220; www.ganjagoddessseattle.com; 3207 1st Ave S; ⏱8am-11pm Mon-Sat, 10am-9pm Sun; 🚋SoDo)

Pink Gorilla Games

VIDEO GAMES

25 🔒 MAP P56, G4

Rare retro games from the old-school Nintendo and Atari days, new releases, toys and collectables – you'll find it all at this neon-pink shop in the International District. Browsing the packed shelves is a fun way to get a nostalgia high, should you have an affinity for the video games of yesteryear. (☎206-547-5790; www.pinkgorillagames.com; 601 S King St; 🚋First Hill Streetcar)

Explore ◈
Belltown &
Seattle Center

Where industry once roared, condos now rise in the thin strip that is Belltown. The neighborhood gained a reputation for trend-setting nightlife in the 1990s; these days it's renowned for its 100-plus restaurants.

It's also near the Seattle Center, home of the Space Needle and former site of the legendary 1962 World's Fair. Today the green lawns attract tourists and families looking for a retreat from downtown.

The Short List

○ *Chihuly Garden & Glass (p70)* Pondering the shimmering glass art that sprang from the creative mind of Dale Chihuly .

○ *Space Needle (p68)* Taking an elevator to the top of the city and marveling at the origins of the innovation and tech boom.

○ *Museum of Pop Culture (p72)* Plugging in a guitar at the Sound Lab and pretending you're Jimi Hendrix.

Getting There & Around

🚌 Dozens of metro buses cross through Belltown, originating from every part of the city.

🚝 The monorail runs every 10 minutes between downtown's Westlake Center and the Seattle Center. Tickets cost $2.50/1.25 per adult/child.

🚶 Lacking busy arterial roads and steep hills, Belltown is a highly walkable neighborhood.

Neighborhood Map on p76

Space Needle (p68)

Top Experiences 📷
Ascend the Space Needle

Whether you're from Cincinnati or Shanghai, your abiding image of Seattle will probably be of the Space Needle, a streamlined, modern-before-its-time tower built for the 1962 World's Fair that has been the city's defining symbol ever since. The needle anchors the Seattle Center and persuades over a million annual visitors to ascend to its flying saucer–like observation deck.

◉ MAP P76, C3

📞 206-905-2100; www.spaceneedle.com

400 Broad St

adult/child $37.50/32.50

🕘 9:30am-11pm Mon-Thu, 9:30am-11:30pm Fri & Sat, 9am-11pm Sun

🚉 Seattle Center

History

The Space Needle (originally called the 'Space Cage') was designed by Victor Steinbrueck and John Graham Jr, reportedly based on the napkin scribblings of World's Fair organizer Eddie Carlson. Looking like a cross between a flying saucer and an hourglass, and belonging to an architectural subgenre commonly referred to as Googie (futuristic, space age and curvaceous), the Needle was constructed in less than a year and proved to be an instant hit; 2.3 million people paid $1 to ascend it during the World's Fair, which ran for six months between April and October 1962.

Rebirth

In 2017, the iconic rotating SkyCity Restaurant was closed as part of a larger face lift, which was unveiled in 2018 and included additions such as the Loupe, a revolving space with glass floors and Atmos Wine Bar (open 1pm to close) wine bar, and an all glass observation deck with inclined benches that provide nearly heart-stopping vistas of the city below.

Visiting

To avoid the queues, purchase your ticket from one of the self-service machines outside the Space Base (tourist shop) and proceed to the elevators. They dock at the **observation deck**. The observation deck has a reasonable cafe (with drinks and sandwiches) inside and a newly renovated glass-walled exterior, which is the real reason to make the trip.

　　Take the spiral staircase called the Oculus down to the Loupe, which is not for those afraid of heights. Although, if you get worked up you can always order a glass of liquid courage at the wine bar.

★ Top Tips

● The Space Needle offers a special day-and-night package (two separate entries) for $59. For a cheaper option, simply ascend half an hour before sunset and linger until it gets dark.

● There are a million ways to photograph the Space Needle in Seattle from locations all over town. Some favorites include: through one of the statues in the Olympic Sculpture Park (p78), or from the Chihuly Garden (p70) looking up.

✖ Take a Break

Head to the lawns around **International Fountain** (Map p76, B2; ☎20 6-684-7200; www. seattlecenter.com; 305 Harrison St; 🚆Seattle Center) for a reprieve from the crowds flocking to the Space Needle.

To avoid overpaying for lunch, step away from the Seattle Center and dine at nearby Tilikum Place Cafe (p80).

Top Experiences 📷

Reflect on the Artworks at Chihuly Garden & Glass

This exquisite exposition of the life and work of dynamic local sculptor Dale Chihuly opened in 2012 and is possibly the finest collection of curated glass art you'll ever see. It shows off Chihuly's creative designs in a suite of interconnected rooms and an adjacent garden in the shadow of the Space Needle.

◎ MAP P76, B3

📞 206-753-4940

www.chihulygardenand
glass.com

305 Harrison St

adult/child $26/17

🕐 10am-8pm Sun-Thu, to 9pm Fri & Sat

🚇 Seattle Center

Exhibition Hall

The first standout exhibit is **Sealife Tower**, a huge azure structure of intricately blown glass that looks as if it has sprung straight out of Poseidon's lair. Look out for the small octopuses and starfish melded into the swirling waves and examine Chihuly's early sketches for the work that adorn the surrounding walls.

The **Ikebana & Float Boat** consists of several boats overflowing with round glass balls and was inspired by Chihuly's time in Venice: he casually threw luminous glass spheres into the canals and watched as local children enthusiastically collected them in boats.

The Glasshouse

Sitting like a giant greenhouse under the Space Needle, the Glasshouse offers a nod to London's erstwhile Crystal Palace, one of Chihuly's most important historical inspirations. You'll notice that the floor space of the glasshouse has been left empty (the area can be hired for wedding receptions), drawing your eye up to the ceiling where a huge medley of flower-shaped glass pieces imitate the reds, oranges and yellows of a perfect sunset.

The Garden

Seattle's relatively benign climate means glass can safely be displayed outside year-round. Chihuly uses the garden to demonstrate the seamless melding of glass art and natural vegetation. Many of the alfresco pieces are simple pointed shards of glass redolent of luminescent reeds, but the real eye-catcher is the **Sun**, a riot of twisted yellow 'flames' whose swirling brilliance erases the heaviness of the most overcast Seattle sky.

★ Top Tips

o Use your Chihuly inspiration to make your own glass art at the nearby **Seattle Glassblowing Studio** (Map p76, E6; 206-448-2181; www.seattleglassblowing.com; 2227 5th Ave; 9am-6pm Mon-Sat, from 10am Sun; 13) in Belltown.

o You can run an audio tour on your cell phone while viewing the exhibits. Simply download it from the museum website.

o If you're also planning to see the other Seattle Center offerings, buy a ticket package to save money.

✕ Take a Break

Get some food away from the museum crowds at the nearby Tilikum Place Cafe (p80).

If all the glass art inspires a desire for cocktails, **Taylor Shellfish Oyster Bar** (Map p76, A1; 206-501-4060; www.taylorshellfishfarms.com; 124 Republican St; oysters $2.75-3.25; 11am-10pm) has you covered.

Top Experiences 📷
Enjoy pop culture at MoPOP

The Museum of Pop Culture (MoPOP) is an inspired marriage between super-modern architecture and legendary rock-and-roll history that sprang from the imagination of Microsoft co-creator Paul Allen (1953–2018). Inside its avant-garde frame, designed by Canadian architect Frank Gehry, you can tune into the famous sounds of Seattle, or attempt to imitate the rock masters in an interactive 'Sound Lab.'

◎ MAP P76, C3

📲 206-770-2700

www.mopop.org

325 5th Ave N

adult/child $28/19

🕙 10am-7pm late May-Aug, 10am-5pm Sep-late May

🖳 Seattle Center

Main Exhibits

The main exhibit hall is anchored by *If VI Was IX* (pictured), a tower of 700 instruments designed by sound sculptor Trimpin. Many of the permanent exhibits center on Hendrix, including the Fender Stratocaster guitar that he played at Woodstock in 1969. There's also a nostalgic slice of grunge memorabilia in a section entitled 'Nirvana: Taking Punk to the Masses'. Dominating proceedings on level 2 is the **Sky Church**, a huge screen displaying musical and sci-fi films.

Sound Lab

Most of the 3rd floor is given over to the interactive Sound Lab, where you can lay down vocal tracks, play instruments, fiddle with effects pedals and – best of all – jam in several ministudios. **On Stage** takes things further, allowing you the opportunity to belt out numbers under stage lights with a virtual audience.

Icons of Science Fiction

A Science Fiction Museum opened here in 2004 and, in 2012, was incorporated into the Museum of Pop Culture in a permanent 2nd-floor exhibit called 'Infinite Worlds of Science Fiction,' displaying artifacts from iconic films and TV shows. Expect to come face to face with a *Doctor Who* Dalek, a *Terminator 2* skull and, more topically, plenty of *Star Wars* life forms and film props.

Architecture

The highly unusual building with its crinkled folds colored in metallic blues and purples was designed by renowned architect Frank Gehry, a strong proponent of deconstructivism. Gehry – who designed the equally outlandish Guggenheim Museum in Bilbao, Spain – supposedly used one of Hendrix's smashed-up guitars as his inspiration.

★ Top Tips

o Save a few buck by getting tickets online.

o Entry to special exhibitions costs extra – but they're a sound investment.

o Tickets last all day, meaning you can leave the complex and re-enter.

o For a great photo, try catching the Space Needle reflected on MoPOP's purple-blue metallic walls.

✕ Take a Break

Adjacent to the museum is the **Seattle Center Armory** (Map p76, B3; 📞206-684-7200; www.seattlecenter.com; 305 Harrison St; ⏰7am-9pm Sun-Thu, to 10pm Fri & Sat; 🚃Seattle Center), which sports a food court full of familiar franchises on its ground floor.

You can get booze and food any time of day at the neighborhood institution 5 Point Café (p81) a few blocks south of the Seattle Center.

Walking Tour 🥾

Strolling Belltown Old & New

Belltown is a neighborhood that has transformed dramatically in the last few decades, to the ire of some and the joy of others. The former lament the days when bolshie bars outnumbered cocktail lounges. The latter claim that, gentrification aside, Belltown is still a rambunctious quarter chock-a-block with bars, restaurants and music venues; it's just the demographic that's altered.

Walk Facts

Start The Moore

End FOB Poke Bar

Length 1.5 miles; two to four hours

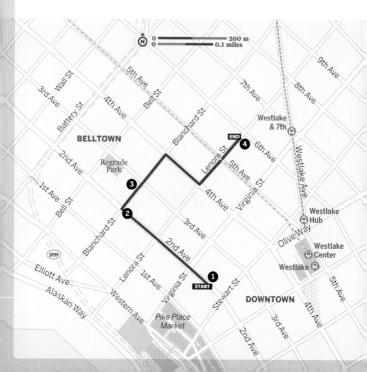

❶ The Moore

There are many reasons why you should start this dip into Belltown's local life at **The Moore**, one of the neighborhood's most iconic haunts. Not only does it possess a great little shoulder-to-shoulder coffee shop, it also harbors the oldest theater in Seattle.

❷ Second Ave Bars

The tight cluster of bars and clubs on this stretch of **2nd Ave** and further is about all that's left of ungentrified Belltown. Options between Blanchard and Virginia Streets on 2nd Ave range from the hip Penny Royal to the craft brews of the **Whisky Bar** (p82) as well as the Jupiter Bar with its arcade machines. If you walk further between Battery and Blanchard Sts you will find even more of what many see as true Old Belltown. Jump into the nocturnal melee of 2nd Ave while it's still rocking.

❸ FOB Poke Bar

FOB Poke Bar (p79) believes in heallthier food with a focus on fresh ingredients catering for all dining choices but be prepared to have to queue at busy times. A key feature is the build-your-own menu where customers choose vegetables or salad and base, such as rice or kale, and then protein, sauce and topping for a very individual dish.

❹ Dimitriou's Jazz Alley

Not a lot of people know it, but Seattle was a hive of jazzy creativity in the 1940s and '50s. Some of the legacy remains, at least in Belltown where **Dimitriou's Jazz Alley** (p82) books national and international jazz acts. This place is a bit of a hidden gem and is a holdout in the face of gentrification of the area. After more than four decades on the scene, it is approaching 'institution' status. It is worth noting that this intimate space is a seated venue but dining is optional.

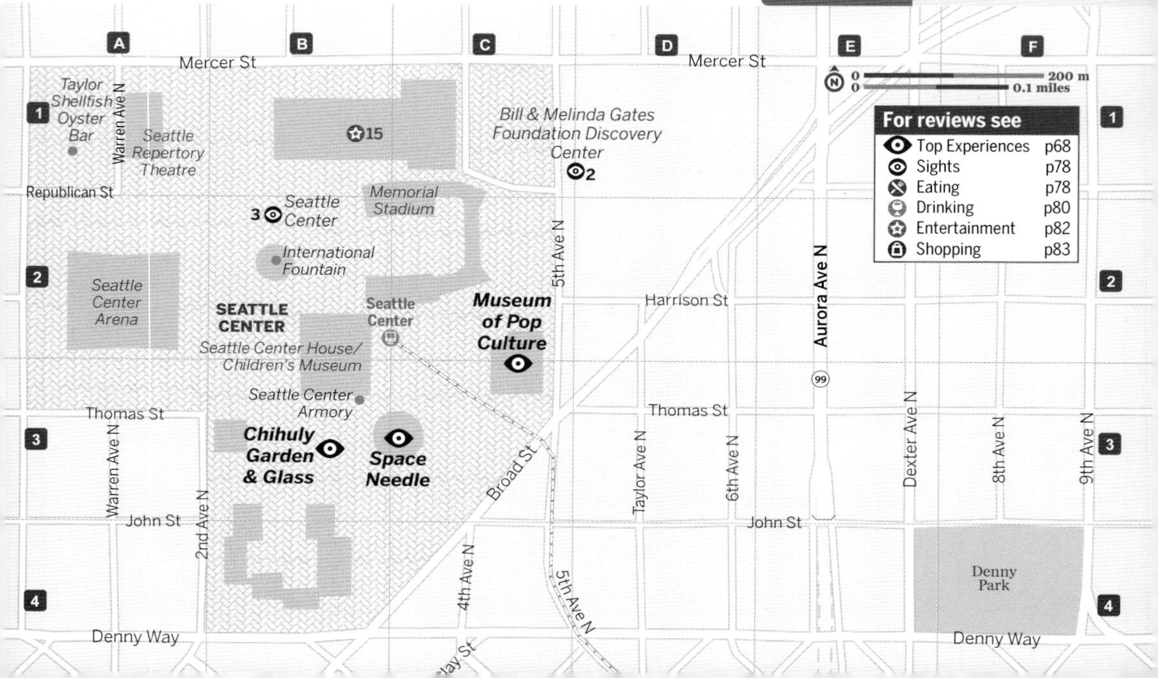

A
B
C
D
E
F
1
2
3
4
Mercer St
Mercer St
Republican St
Harrison St
Thomas St
Thomas St
John St
John St
Denny Way
Denny Way
Warren Ave N
Warren Ave N
2nd Ave N
4th Ave N
5th Ave N
5th Ave N
Taylor Ave N
6th Ave N
Aurora Ave N
99
Dexter Ave N
8th Ave N
9th Ave N
Broad St
Taylor Shellfish Oyster Bar
Seattle Repertory Theatre
Seattle Center Arena
15
3 Seattle Center
International Fountain
Memorial Stadium
SEATTLE CENTER
Seattle Center
Seattle Center House/ Children's Museum
Seattle Center Armory
Chihuly Garden & Glass
Space Needle
Museum of Pop Culture
Bill & Melinda Gates Foundation Discovery Center
2
Denny Park
0 200 m
0 0.1 miles
For reviews see
Top Experiences p68
Sights p78
Eating p78
Drinking p80
Entertainment p82
Shopping p83

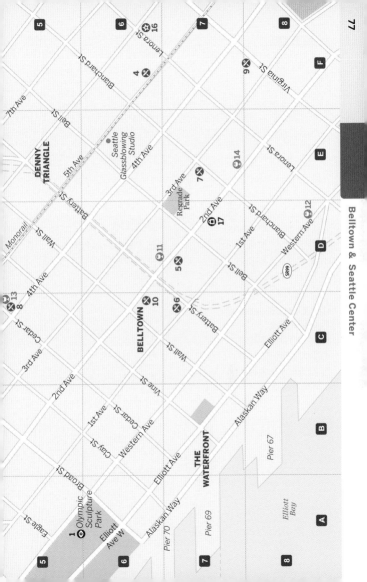

5

6

16

4

7

8

F

9

7th Ave

Bell St

Blanchard St

Lenora St

DENNY
TRIANGLE

5th Ave

Seattle
Glassblowing
Studio

4th Ave

Battery St

Virginia St

Lenora St

E

3rd Ave
Regrade
Park

7

2nd Ave

17

Blanchard St

14

Monorail

Wall St

11

1st Ave

5

Western Ave

12

Bell St

D

SR99

4th Ave

13
8

Cedar St

10

Wall St

6

BELLTOWN

Battery St

Elliott Ave

C

3rd Ave

2nd Ave

Vine St

B

1st Ave

Cedar St

Clay St

Western Ave

Alaskan Way

THE
WATERFRONT

Pier 67

Broad St

Olympic
Sculpture
Park

Elliott
Ave W

Elliott Ave

Alaskan Way

Pier 69

Elliott
Bay

A

Eagle St

1

Pier 70

8

7

6

5

Sights

Olympic Sculpture Park

PARK

1 ⊙ MAP P76, A5

This ingenuous feat of urban planning is an official offshoot of the Seattle Art Museum and bears the same strong eye toward design and curation. There are over 20 sculptures to admire in this green space that sprawls out over reclaimed urban decay. You can also enjoy them in passing while traversing the park's winding trails. Views of the Puget Sound and Olympic Peninsula in the background will delight anyone looking for some great pictures for social media. (☎206-654-3100; 2901 Western Ave; admission free; ⊙sunrise-sunset; ☐33)

Bill & Melinda Gates Foundation Discovery Center

VISITOR CENTER

2 ⊙ MAP P76, D1

The work of the Bill & Melinda Gates Foundation is celebrated at this suitably high-tech visitor center, part of a larger foundation building located opposite the Space Needle. Spread over five rooms with highly interactive exhibits, the center lays out the Gates' bios and shows examples of their work around the world, including fighting malaria in Africa and notable philanthropic activities inside the US. (☎206-709-3100; www.discovergates.org; 440 5th Ave N; admission free; ⊙10am-5pm Tue-Sat; ☐Seattle Center)

Seattle Center

LANDMARK

3 ⊙ MAP P76, B2

The remnants of the futuristic 1962 World's Fair hosted by Seattle and subtitled Century 21 Exposition are still visible over 50 years later at the Seattle Center. Thanks to regular upgrades, the complex has retained its luster and contains Seattle's highest concentration of A-list sights. It's also a superb green space close to downtown. (☎206-684-8582; www.seattlecenter. com; 400 Broad St; ☐Seattle Center)

Eating

Top Pot Hand-Forged Doughnuts

CAFE $

4 ✗ MAP P76, F6

Sitting pretty in a glass-fronted former car showroom with art deco signage and immense bookshelves, Top Pot's flagship cafe produces the Ferraris of the doughnut world. It might have morphed into a 20-outlet chain but its hand-molded collection of sweet rings are still – arguably – some of the best in the city. The coffee's pretty potent too. (www. toppotdoughnuts.com; 2124 5th Ave; doughnuts from $1.29; ⊙6am-7pm Mon-Fri, 7am-7pm Sat & Sun; ☐13)

Tavolàta

ITALIAN $$$

5 ✗ MAP P76, D7

Owned by top Seattle chef Ethan Stowell, Tavolàta is a dinner-only, Italian-inspired eatery emphasizing homemade pasta dishes and hearty

Olympic Sculpture Park

mains like a rack of wild boar with fig *mostarda* (a sweet and spicy mustard and fruit sauce). Many consider it among the best Italian spots in the city. (📞206-838-8008; 2323 2nd Ave; mains $18-32; ⏱5-11pm; 🚍13)

Macrina   BAKERY $

6 ⊗ MAP P76, C7

That snaking queue's there for a reason: damned good artisanal bread (you can watch through the window as the experts roll out the dough). There are two options and two lines at Macrina. One is for the fantastic take-out bakery (possibly the best in Seattle); the other's for the sit-down cafe with its so-good-it-could-be-Paris sandwiches, soups and other such snacks.

(📞206-448-4032; www.macrinabak ery.com; 2408 1st Ave; sandwiches $6.50-10.50; ⏱7am-6pm; 🚍13)

FOB Poke Bar   POKE $

7 ⊗ MAP P76, E7

Ultrafresh ingredients and bold fla- vors have made relative Belltown newcomer FOB Poke Bar an in- stant success in the casual dining scene. This is a make-your-own- bowl place where you can go the simple salmon or tuna route, or mix things up with ingredients like spam and octopus. If you come during lunch hours, be prepared to queue. (📞206-728-9888; www.fob pokebar.com; 220 Blanchard St; poke bowls from $11; ⏱11am-10pm; 🚍13)

It Happened at the World's Fair

Known officially as the Century 21 Exposition, Seattle's 1962 World's Fair set out to depict the future, as envisaged through the eyes of an affluent Cold War generation. The fair attracted 10 million visitors, including a freshly demobbed Elvis Presley in the throes of a skin-crawlingly trite movie career. His movie *It Happened at the World's Fair* was partly filmed in Seattle and dubbed a lemon by critics. Luckily the fair itself garnered more plaudits and turned a tidy profit. It also helped cement Seattle as a top-tier American city.

Tilikum Place Cafe   BISTRO $$$

8 ✶ MAP P76, C5

This charmer of a European-style cafe is beloved by locals for lunch (sardine sandwiches) and brunch (Dutch baby pancakes) and dinner (roasted chicken with Yukon potatoes) and dessert (chocolate polenta cake) – don't make them choose. You'll find it packed no matter the time of day, and it's one of the best dining options within spitting distance of the Space Needle. (☏206-282-4830; www.tilikumplacecafe.com; 407 Cedar St; brunch mains $9-14, dinner mains $23-32; ☉11am-3pm & 5-10pm Mon-Fri, 8am-3pm & 5-10pm Sat & Sun; ☒3)

Serious Pie   PIZZA $$

9 ✶ MAP P76, F8

In the crowded confines of Serious Pie you can enjoy beautifully blistered pizza bases topped with such unconventional ingredients as clams, potatoes, nettles, soft eggs, truffle cheese and more. Be prepared to share a table and meet a few Seattleites. (☏206-838-7388; www.seriouspieseattle.com; 316 Virginia St; pizzas $17-19; ☉11am-11pm; ☒South Lake Union Streetcar)

La Vita é Bella   ITALIAN $$

10 ✶ MAP P76, C6

As any Italian food snob will tell you, it's very hard to find authentic home-spun Italian cuisine this side of Sicily. Thus extra kudos must go to La Vita é Bella for trying and largely succeeding in a difficult field. The pizza margherita is a good yardstick, though the *vongole* (clams), desserts and coffee are also spot on. (☏206-441-5322; 2411 2nd Ave; pasta $15-23; ☉11:30am-3pm & 5-10pm Mon-Thu, to 11pm Fri & Sat, 5-10pm Sun; ☒13)

Drinking

Rendezvous   BAR

11 ☕ MAP P76, D6

Rendezvous is one of Belltown's oldest heirlooms, starting life in 1927 as a speakeasy and a screening room for early Hollywood talkies. Now on its umpteenth incarnation, the subterranean speakeasy has morphed into 'the Grotto' (with weekly comedy), the screening room has become the diminutive **Jewel Box Theater** and the clamorous space upstairs a chic-ish bar and restaurant. (📞20 6-441-5823; www.rendezvous.rocks; 2320 2nd Ave; 🕓4pm-2am; 🚌13)

Cloudburst Brewing

MICROBREWERY

12 🔲 MAP P76, D8

The brainchild of former experimental brewer at Elysian Brewing, Steve Luke, Cloudburst Brewing became an instant Seattle favorite. Replicating the success of Luke's past brewing creations, Cloudburst Brewing features hoppy beers with sassy names, and the bare-bones

tasting room is always packed to the gills with beer fans who want to support craft beer in Seattle. (📞20 6-602-6061; www.cloudburstbrew.com; 2116 Western Ave; 🕓2-10pm Wed-Fri, noon-10pm Sat & Sun; 🚌13)

5 Point Café

BAR

13 🔲 MAP P76, C5

There are Belltown relics and then there's the 5 Point whose seedy neon sign and cantankerous advertising blurb ('cheating tourists and drunks since 1929') is practically as iconic as the Space Needle – and 33 years older! Half-diner, half-bar and too worn-in to be mistaken for hip, it's where seasoned Charles Bukowski look-alikes go to get wasted. (📞206-448-9993; www.the5pointcafe.com; 415 Cedar St; 🕓24hr; 🚌3)

The Moore, (p75)

Whisky Bar

BAR

14 🚇 MAP P76, E7

This spot is about more than just the whiskey, though that, of course, is good. If you're sticking to home turf, try the locally made Westland single malt. There are genuine British food treats as well. Where else in Seattle can you get Welsh rarebit – or Scotch eggs for that matter? (📞206-443-4490; www.thewhiskybar.com; 2122 2nd Ave; 🕐noon-2am; 🚌13)

Entertainment

McCaw Hall

OPERA

15 ⭐ MAP P76, B1

Home of the **Seattle Opera** (www.seattleopera.org) and the **Pacific Northwest Ballet** (www.pnb.

org), McCaw Hall is another venue which was developed as part of the Seattle Fair of 1962. This magnificent structure in the Seattle Center was given a massive overhaul in 2003. (📞206-684-7200; www.mccawhall.com; 321 Mercer St; 🚇Seattle Center)

Dimitriou's Jazz Alley

JAZZ

16 ⭐ MAP P76, F6

Hidden in an unlikely spot behind a boring-looking office building is Seattle's most sophisticated and prestigious jazz club. Dimitriou's hosts the best of the locals, as well as many national and international acts passing through. (📞206-441-9729; www.jazzalley.com; 2033 6th Ave; 🕐shows 7:30pm & 9:30pm; 🚋South Lake Union Streetcar)

McCaw Hall

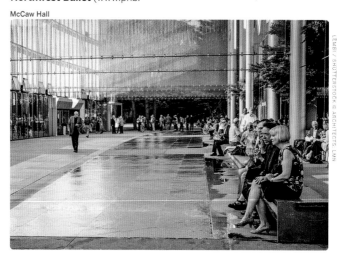

Belltown's Storied History

This area was named after William Nathaniel Bell, one of the original settlers who owned the land on which the district was developed. Originally a hilly area it was levelled in the late 1800s. A movie industry sprouted up in the early 1900s and low-cost spaces attracted artists in the 1970s.

By the mid-1980s Belltown was a featureless amalgam of dull warehouses and low-rise office blocks. Offering cheap rents and ample studio space, it became an escape hatch for underground musicians and artists and led, in part, to the spark that ignited grunge. This century, development has seen massive change in the area with high-rise glass towers now abutting old Belltown.

Shopping

Singles Going Steady   MUSIC

17 🔒 MAP P76, D7

Singles Going Steady – named after an album by British punk pioneers the Buzzcocks – is a niche record store specializing in punk, Oi!, reggae and ska, mostly in the form of 7-inch vinyl singles, as well as posters, patches and other accessories. There's a good little magazine selection too. (📞206-441-7396; 2219 2nd Ave; ⏰noon-7pm Tue-Thu, to 8pm Fri & Sat, to 6pm Sun; 🚌13)

Queen Anne & Lake Union

Queen Anne is a neighborhood double bill: the top of the hill hoards beautiful early-20th-century mansions (as well as spectacular views), while the bottom features a more egalitarian mix of solid restaurants and cafes. Nearby Lake Union's southern shores are changing more quickly than the influx of techies can tweet about them.

The Short List

○ **Museum of History & Industry (p86)** *Riding the streetcar to this fabulous museum for a first-class exposition of Seattle's grunge-playing, aircraft-building, computer-designing history.*

○ **Cheshiahud Loop (p92)** *Circumnavigating Lake Union on foot (or bike) on this well-signposted 6-mile route that will take you through multiple waterfront neighborhoods.*

○ **Kerry Park (p92)** *Viewing lakes, islands, skyscrapers and the even more sky-scraping Mt Rainier from this spectacular lookout at sunset, amid Beverly Hills–like mansions.*

Getting There & Around

🚌 Metro buses 2 and 13 run frequently to Queen Anne from downtown and Seattle Center. Buses 62 and 70 serve the Westlake and Eastlake neighborhoods of Lake Union from downtown.

🚋 One of Seattle's two main streetcar lines runs between South Lake Union (SLU) and the Westlake Center in downtown every 10 minutes.

Neighborhood Map on p90

The Burke-Gilman Trail (p18) DIEGOMEZR / SHUTTERSTOCK ©

Top Experiences 📷

Time Travel at the Museum of History & Industry

Almost everything you need to know about Seattle is crammed into the fabulous Museum of History & Industry (MOHAI), located in plush digs on the southern shore of Lake Union. In operation since the 1950s, and with an archive of over four million objects, MOHAI displays its stash of historical booty in an impressively repurposed naval armory building.

⊙ MAP P90, F4

📞 206-324-1126

www.mohai.org

860 Terry Ave N

adult/child under 14yr
$19.95/free

🕙 10am-5pm; ♿

🚋 South Lake Union
Streetcar

Interactive Exhibits

The big eye-catcher as you walk into the huge hangar-sized space is a 1919 **Boeing airplane** hanging from the roof – the first commercial Boeing ever made. Indeed, the name 'Boeing' looms large over the whole museum, along with numerous other Seattle icons (Starbucks, Rainier beer, grunge). In the city that produced Microsoft, there is no shortage of interactive exhibits to enjoy, including a photo and comment booth, touchscreen TVs and an opportunity to explore railroad history by banging large mallets on railway sleepers. Kids will have a ball. With so many artifacts to call upon, exhibits change regularly, although the museum's overriding sentiment remains constant: an unashamed celebration of Seattle's short but action-packed history.

Upper Floors

On the upper floors, rooms are arranged around a mezzanine with the exhibits unfolding chronologically, using various themes to paint a multilayered portrait of the city room by room. Highlights include the engineering feats of early Native American settlers, the 1889 Great Fire, the 1962 World's Fair, a focus on film and TV (covering everything from *Twin Peaks* to *Grey's Anatomy*), the city's vibrant LGBTIQ+ community and an interesting dip into Seattle's counterculture – including a self-critical look at the 1999 WTO conference riots. A short but attention-grabbing film in a purpose-built theater advertises Seattle in all its scenic and musical splendor. Regularly changing temporary shows are also a feature; 'Seattle Style: Function/Fashion' and 'Agents of Change: 20 Remarkable Jewish Women of Washington State' are stand-out previous examples.

On the top floor there's an ingenious **periscope** that offers visitors a 360-degree view of the world outside, dominated by the glistening waters of Lake Union.

★ Top Tips

○ The museum offers free entry on the first Thursday of every month between 10am and 8pm.

○ Ditch the car (SLU is notorious for roadworks). Outside the museum there's a tram stop (10 minutes to downtown), a bike-share docking station, or – if you're intrepid – a boat moorage.

✕ Take a Break

Give yourself a post-museum caffeine boost at Citizen Coffee (p94), a few blocks away.

If you need something more substantial, join the business lunch crowd at **El Grito** (Map p90, G5; ☏ 206-659-4552; www.elgritoseattle .com; 234 Fairview Ave N; mains $11-16; ⊙ 11am-10pm Mon-Thu, to 1am Fri, 10am-1am Sat, 10am-4pm Sun; ⎘ South Lake Union Streetcar).

Walking Tour 🥾

Queen Anne Coffee Crawl

*Queen Anne is a microcosm of Seattle's famously
fertile coffee scene. It's not coincidental that quite
a few of the city's coffee chains opened up their
first cafes here. To experience the best of the
best in caffeine-infused drinks and mingle among
coffee-addicted locals with discerning palates,
head out of Belltown on Queen Anne Ave N and
keep walking.*

Walk Facts

Start Lower Queen Anne

End Caffe Fiore

Length 1 mile; two hours

❶ Lower Queen Anne

Hungry tourists from the Seattle Center bump into affluent young techies on their breaks in Lower Queen Anne (or 'Uptown' as it's also known), the thin strip at the bottom of the hill that strikes a less haughty pose than its lofty neighbor. Uptown is locally renowned for its eclectic mix of economical restaurants and coffee shops.

❷ Uptown Espresso Bar

It's all about the foam at **Uptown Espresso Bar** (📞206-285-3757; https://velvetfoam.com; 525 Queen Anne Ave N; 🕐6am-6pm; 📶; 🚌13). It's legendarily velvety, which helped turn this original Lower Queen Anne coffee house into a city-wide chain that, unlike Starbucks, locals still rave about en masse.

❸ Mecca Café

You can choose your poison in **Mecca Café** (📞206-285-9728; http://mecca-cafe.com; 526 Queen Anne Ave N; burgers from $10.50; 🕐7am-2am; 🚌13), Lower Queen Anne's dive bar of choice – for caffeine or alcohol. Half of the skinny room is a ketchup-on-the-table diner, the other side is a dive bar where the beer mats are as tattooed as the customers. Opened at the tail-end of prohibition, it's been a reliable spreader of local gossip since 1930.

❹ Caffe Ladro

After Mecca, **Ladro** (📞206-282-5313; www.caffeladro.com; 2205 Queen Anne Ave N; 🕐5:30am-8pm Mon-Fri, 6am-8pm Fri & Sat; 📶; 🚌13) is positively refined. The Seattle-only coffee chain not only roasts its own beans, it also bakes its own pastries. For a double whammy of bitter and sweet, place your order in the cozy corner cafe and give yourself enough rocket fuel to climb the Counterbalance, the steep hill that starts just outside the door.

❺ Caffè Fiore

You're more likely to detect the aroma of coffee than *fiore* (flowers) in tucked-away neighborhood staple **Caffè Fiore** (📞206-282-1441; www.caffefiore.com; 224 W Galer St; 🕐6am-6pm; 🚌2), one of several Seattle coffee chainlets that opened their first cafe in Queen Anne. The 'Sevilla' – a mocha with orange zest – is a genuine sensation.

A

B

C

D

1

W Crockett St

8

Boston St

15

5th Ave W
4th Ave W
3rd Ave W
2nd Ave W

10

W Howe St

1st Ave N
Warren Ave N
2nd Ave N

Newton St

Bigelow Ave N
5th Ave N

6th Ave W

W Blaine St

QUEEN
ANNE

Queen Anne Ave N
1st Ave N

Blaine St

3rd Ave N
Nob Hill Ave N
4th Ave N

2

W Garfield St

Hayes St

20

Garfield St

Taylor Ave N

13

W Galer St

Galer St

W Lee St

Lee St

3rd Ave N

6th Ave W

W Comstock St

Bigelow Ave N

Bhy
Kracke
Park

3

W Highland Dr

4 Kerry Park

Highland Dr

W Prospect St

3rd Ave W
2nd Ave W
1st Ave W

Prospect St

4th Ave N

Ward St

Kinnear
Park

W Olympic Pl

1st Ave N
Warren Ave N
2nd Ave N
3rd Ave N

Aloha St

5th Ave N
Taylor Ave N

4

W Roy St

17

Valley St

16

11

6th Ave W
5th Ave W
4th Ave W

7

Roy St

Mercer St

LOWER
QUEEN ANNE

W Republican St

Seattle
Repertory
Theatre

McCaw
Hall

14

Elliott Ave W

Queen Anne Ave N

W Harrison St

2nd Ave W
1st Ave N

Seattle
Center
Arena

SEATTLE
CENTER

Memorial
Stadium

Seattle
Center

5

Museum of
Pop Culture

Thomas St

Children's
Theater

Space
Needle

Broad St

6

Elliott
Bay

Myrtle
Edwards
Park

Denny Way

A

B

C

D

Queen Anne & Lake Union

E

F

G

H

Northwest Outdoor Center

6

E Boston St

9

E Newton St

8th Ave N

Westlake Ave N

Fairview Ave E

Minor Ave E

Yale Ave E

EASTLAKE

Eastlake Ave E

500 m
0.25 miles

For reviews see

Top Experiences p86
Sights p92
Eating p93
Drinking p95
Entertainment p96
Shopping p97

WESTLAKE

E Galer St

Aurora Ave N

Dexter Ave N

Cheshiahud Loop

Lake
Union
1

Fairview Ave N

Lakeview Blvd E

6th Ave N

Aloha St

Valley St

Roy St

Westlake Ave N

8th Ave N

Lake
Union
Park

2

5

*Museum of
History &
Industry*

Center for
Wooden Boats

Fairview
& Campus
Drive

Valley St

CAPITOL
HILL

E Roy St

Cheshiahud
Loop

Valley St

3

Lake Union Park

Westlake
& Mercer

Terry &
Mercer

Mercer St

E Mercer St

Broad St

Republican St

9th Ave N

Westlake Ave N

Terry Ave N

Boren Ave N

SOUTH
LAKE
UNION

Minor Ave N

Pontius Ave N

Yale Ave N

Eastlake Ave E

Melrose Ave E

Bellevue Ave E

Summit Ave E

Belmont Ave E

12

Harrison St

Harrison St

Thomas St Westlake &
Thomas

Terry &
Thomas

Cascade
Playground

Thomas St

El Grito

19

Denny
Park

John St

18

Westlake
& 9th

Denny Way

E Olive Way

E

F

G

H

Sights

Lake Union

LAKE

1 ◎ MAP P90, F3

Unifying Seattle's various bodies of water, freshwater Lake Union was carved by glacial erosion 12,000 years ago. Native American Duwamish tribes once subsisted on its then-isolated shores, but 21st-century Lake Union is backed by densely packed urban neighborhoods and is linked to both Lake Washington and Puget Sound by the Lake Washington Ship Canal, built as part of a huge engineering project in the 1910s. (🚋 South Lake Union Streetcar)

Lake Union Park

PARK

2 ◎ MAP P90, F4

Opened in 2010, this welcome green patch occupies ex-navy land on the southern tip of Lake Union and has a wading pond (with model sailboats you can use), an attractive bridge and a boat launch. It hosts the Museum of History & Industry (p86) in the old naval armory building and the Center for Wooden Boats. (📞 206-684-4075; 860 Terry Ave N; ⏰ 4am-11:30pm; 🚻; 🚋 South Lake Union Streetcar)

Cheshiahud Loop

WALKING, RUNNING

3 ◎ MAP P90, F4

Inaugurated years ago to tie in with the landscaping of Lake Union Park, this well-signposted 6-mile route circumnavigates Lake Union by gelling together existing trails, sidewalks and paths. Named for a Duwamish chief who once headed a lakeside village, it's a good way to keep away from busy roads while walking/jogging/cycling through at least five Seattle neighborhoods. (📞 206-684-4075; www.seattle.gov/parks; Westlake Ave N & Valley St; ⏰ 4am-11:30pm; 🚋 South Lake Union Streetcar)

Kerry Park

PARK, VIEWPOINT

4 ◎ MAP P90, B3

Amid the glittering Beverly Hills–like homes of Highland Dr, mere commoners can enjoy eagle's-eye views of downtown Seattle and Elliott Bay (and Mt Rainier, should it take off its cloudy hat) from this spectacular lookout. (📞 206-684-4075; 211 W Highland Dr; ⏰ 6am-10pm; 🚻; 🚌 2)

Center for Wooden Boats

MUSEUM

5 ◎ MAP P90, F4

Honoring Seattle's historical, aquatic and Native American antecedents, this one-of-a-kind museum and enthusiasts' center features vintage and replica boats and offers rentals. Best of all, however, are its free Sunday public sailboat rides on Lake Union – first come, first served; sign-ups start 10am. (📞 206-382-2628; www.cwb.org; 1010 Valley St; sailboat/rowboat/kayak rental per hr $40/40/35; ⏰ museum 10am-8pm Tue-Sun, rentals from 1pm; 🚻; 🚋 South Lake Union Streetcar)

Upper Queen Anne

Sitting on a 456ft hill above the Seattle Center, Queen Anne proper is an elegant collection of majestic redbrick houses and apartment buildings, sweeping lawns manicured to perfection, and gorgeous views of the city and Elliott Bay. Vistas aside (and, yes, they're worth the energy expenditure), the favorite pastime here is 'mansion-viewing,' ie wandering at will along the traffic-lite streets spying on an opulent array of fin de siècle architecture.

Northwest Outdoor Center
KAYAKING

6 MAP P90, E1

Located on the west side of Lake Union, this place rents kayaks and stand-up paddleboards (SUPs) and offers tours and instruction in sea and white-water kayaking. (☏206-281-9694; www.nwoc.com; 2100 Westlake Ave N; kayak/SUP rental per hr $18/20; ⏰10am-8pm Mon-Fri, 9am-6pm Sat & Sun Apr-Sep, closed Mon & Tue Oct-Mar; 🚌62)

Eating

Toulouse Petit
CAJUN, CREOLE $$

7 ✖ MAP P90, B4

Hailed for its generous happy hours, cheap brunches and rollicking atmosphere, this busy Queen Anne eatery has the common touch. The menu is large and varied, offering choices such as blackened rib-eye steak, freshwater gulf prawns and house-made gnocchi with artichoke hearts. (☏206-432-9069; www.toulousepetit.com; 601 Queen Anne Ave N; dinner mains $17-45; ⏰9am-2am Mon-Fri, from 8am Sat & Sun; 🚌13)

How to Cook a Wolf
ITALIAN $$

8 ✖ MAP P90, B1

Despite its scary name, the Ethan Stowell-run HTCAW has nothing to do with roasting wild fauna over your campfire. Rather it's poached from a book written by MFK Fisher during wartime rationing about how to make the most of limited ingredients. Though times have changed, Stowell embraces the same philosophy. (☏206-838-8090; www.ethanstowellrestaurants.com; 2208 Queen Anne Ave N; pasta $19-23; ⏰5-11pm; 🚌13)

Serafina
ITALIAN $$

9 ✖ MAP P90, H1

This lovely neighborhood Italian restaurant in Eastlake specializes in regional Tuscan-style cooking, with simply prepared meat and fish, as well as pastas that can be ordered as a first or main course. A gorgeous leafy deck area behind the restaurant doubles as the entryway to **Cicchetti**, Serafina's sister restaurant, which serves Mediterranean snacks. Reservations at Serafina are recommended.

Dining in South Lake Union

The area around Lake Union used to be a culinary wasteland, but how things have changed, especially in South Lake Union. Big-name chefs such as Tom Douglas have moved in to cater for the neighborhood's many affluent businesses and residents. Places tend to get busy at lunchtime on weekdays and during after-work happy hours.

(206-323-0807; www.serafinaseattle.com; 2043 Eastlake Ave E; pastas $16-18, mains $24-36; 5-10pm Sun & Mon, 11:30am-2:30pm & 5-10pm Tue-Thu, to 11pm Fri, 5-11pm Sat; 70)

Canlis   AMERICAN $$$

10 MAP P90, D1

One of Seattle's most celebrated restaurants, Canlis is old-school posh and one of the few places in the city where people regularly get dressed up for dinner (as per the restaurant's dress code). The menu is Pacific Northwest tradi-tional (halibut, pork, fresh veg) and the decor's like something out of a 1950s-era Hitchcock movie – all angled glass and sweeping views. (206-283-3313; https://canlis.com; 2576 Aurora Ave N; 4-course dinner $135; 5:30pm-late Mon-Sat; 5)

Citizen Coffee   SANDWICHES, BREAKFAST $

11 MAP P90, D4

Citizen serves breakfast until 4pm and it's a good one. There are plenty of options at this popular redbrick joint near the Space Needle, where you can opt for Greek yogurt and fruit, biscuits and gravy, or huevos rancheros. The slightly tucked-away location means it's less tourist-heavy and more local. (206-284-1015; www.citizencoffee.com; 706 Taylor Ave N; mains $7-13; 7am-9pm Mon-Sat, to 3:30pm Sun; 3)

Serious Biscuit   AMERICAN $

12 MAP P90, F5

After Serious Pie (p80) comes Serious Biscuit, Tom Douglas' first bite at the South Lake Union cookie that has lured so many restaurants into the neighborhood in the 2010s The buttery biscuits serve as flaky bases to a variety of brunch-worthy toppings – the 'zach' (fried chicken, gravy, bacon and egg) is a perennial favorite. (206-436-0050; www.seriouspie-attle.com/westlake; 401 Westlake Ave N; biscuits $8-13; 7am-3pm Mon-Fri, 9am-3pm Sat & Sun; South Lake Union Streetcar)

5 Spot   BREAKFAST $$

13 MAP P90, B2

Top of the hill, top of the morning and top of the brunch charts: the queues outside 5 Spot at 10am on a Sunday are testament to its popularity. The crowds inspire a great atmosphere, and the hearty menu, with its perfect French toast, huevos rancheros and plenty more American standards, will shift the stubbornest of hangovers. (www.chowfoods.com; 1502 Queen Anne Ave N; ⏾8am-11pm Mon-Fri, 8am-3pm & 5pm-midnight Sat & Sun; 🛗; 🚌2)

Drinking

Holy Mountain Brewing Company MICROBREWERY

14 🗺 MAP P90, A5

A newer brewery with a handful of years under its belt, Holy Mountain has developed a serious cult following. Focused on ales aged in oak barrels and an ever-changing lineup of new taps, Holy Mountain offers beer lovers a taste of something a bit different. (www.holymountainbrewing.com; 1421 Elliott Ave W; ⏾3-9pm Mon-Thu, noon-10pm Fri & Sat, to 9pm Sun; 🚌RapidRide D Line)

Hilltop Ale House PUB

15 🗺 MAP P90, B1

Hilltop Ale House is a comfy neighborhood hangout on Queen Anne Hill, sister to the **74th Street Ale House** (www.74thst.com; 7401 Greenwood Ave N; ⏾11am-11pm Sun-Thu, to midnight Fri & Sat; 🚌5) in Phinney Ridge. It has a friendly vibe and a large selection of microbrews, served in proper 20oz pints, and the menu is well above your standard pub fare, with mains $11 to $15. (📞206-723-5123;

Centre for Wooden Boats (p92)

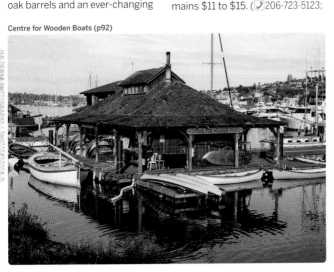

REI (p97)

www.seattlealehouses.com; 2129 Queen Anne Ave N; ⊘11am-11pm Sun-Thu, to midnight Fri & Sat; 🚍13)

McMenamins Queen Anne

MICROBREWERY

16 🚇 MAP P90, C4

The McMenamin brothers' micro-brewing empire is a product of Portland, OR, but you can enjoy a comforting out-of-state taste of the brand's ever-successful blend of psychedelia meets art nouveau meets wood-paneled gentleman's club at this Lower Queen Anne perch. The real draw, of course, is the beer, including the classic Hammerhead pale ale, loaded with Oregon hops. It's kid-friendly.

(📞206-285-4722; www.mcmenamins. com; 200 Roy St; ⊘11am-midnight Mon-Thu, to 1am Fri & Sat, noon-midnight Sun; 👪; 🚍13)

Entertainment

On the Boards

DANCE, THEATER

17 ⭐ MAP P90, B4

The place for avant-garde performance art, the nonprofit On the Boards makes its home at the intimate Behnke Center for Contemporary Performance and showcases some innovative and occasionally weird dance and music. (📞206-217-9886; www.

ontheboards.org; 100 W Roy St; tickets from $10; 🚌13)

El Corazon — LIVE MUSIC

18 ⭐ MAP P90, G6

Formerly going by the names of the Off-Ramp, then Graceland, El Corazon has lots of history echoing around its walls – and lots of sweaty, beer-drenched bodies bouncing off them. Save your clean shirt for another night, and don't expect perfect sound quality at every show. The gutsy bands play loudly, presumably to drown out the traffic noise from I-5 just outside the door. (📞206-262-0482; www.elcorazonseattle.com; 109 Eastlake Ave E; 🚌70)

Shopping

REI — OUTDOOR EQUIPMENT

19 🔒 MAP P90, G6

REI is the be-all and end-all of outdoor clothing and equipment, and its Lake Union flagship is no exception. In fact, it even comes with additional perks like an outdoor mountain-bike test track. The store also rents various ski packages, climbing gear and camping equipment, and organizes a ton of courses from map-reading to bike maintenance. (📞206-223-1944; www.rei.com; 222 Yale Ave N; 🕐9am-9pm Mon-Sat, 10am-7pm Sun; 🚌70)

Queen Anne Book Company — BOOKS

20 🔒 MAP P90, B2

This charming little nook is everything a neighborhood bookstore should be, with frequent poetry readings and book signings. Adjoining coffee shop **El Diablo** (www.eldiablocoffee.com; 🕐6am-6pm; 📶) has a lovely little patio where you can sip a coffee and pore over your latest book purchase. (📞206-283-5624; www.qabookco.com; 1811 Queen Anne Ave N; 🕐10am-7pm Mon-Fri, to 5pm Sat & Sun; 🚌13)

Walking Tour 🚶

Lake Washington Parks & Pubs

The neighborhoods on Seattle's east side rarely get out-of-town visitors. If you're bored of sightseeing or were unable to uncover the soul of Seattle despite multiple visits to the Space Needle, make a trip to some of the tucked-away parks that overlook Lake Washington. A smattering of local pubs plug the gaps in between.

Getting There

🚌 Metro bus 11 runs from downtown along E Madison St all the way to Madison Park. Buses 2 and 3 connect downtown with Madrona via Capitol Hill.

❶ Madison Park Neighborhood

If the weather's good, **Madison Park**'s charming beach-town vibe makes it worth visiting. It is best reached on bus 11 along E Madison St, following an old trolley line that once bused in knackered lumber workers for some weekend R and R.

❷ Attic Alehouse & Eatery

Decades ago, this Madison Park boozer overlooking the beach was a shooting gallery/bowling alley combo. It first became a restaurant in the mid-1930s, then a tavern in the '50s. The current 1960s-vintage building has morphed into friendly neighborhood pub **Attic Alehouse** (☎206-323-3131; www.atticalehouseseattle.com; 4226 E Madison St; ⊗11am-2am Mon-Fri, 9am-2am Sat & Sun; 🚍11).

❸ Denny Blaine Park

After soaking up Madison Park, head a few blocks south to one of several lesser known 'hidden' parks that abut Lake Washington. **Denny Blaine Park** (☎206-684-4075; 200 Lake Washington Blvd E; ⊗6am-10pm; 🚍2) sits at the end of a looping tree-lined lane, and its more secluded location amid the luxury piles of lakeside millionaires means it sometimes attracts nude or seminude sunbathers.

❹ Viretta Park

Amid a lakeside nirvana of posh mansions and a few blocks south of Denny Blaine sits two-tiered **Viretta Park** (☎206-684-4075; 151 Lake Washington Blvd E; admission free; ⊗4am-11:30pm; 🚍2), whose two graffiti-covered park benches have been adopted as Seattle's unofficial Kurt Cobain memorial. The large house in which the Nirvana singer took his life in April 1994 is on the park's north side.

❺ Hi Spot Café

The **Hi Spot Café** (☎206-325-7905; www.hispotcafe.com; 1410 34th Ave; mains $10-14; ⊗7am-4pm Mon-Fri, from 8am Sat & Sun; 🚍2) is a comfy little space in an old craftsman-style house in Madrona where you can either get a sit-down meal (brunch is best) or a quick espresso and pastry to go. Regulars recommend the humongous cinnamon buns.

❻ Madrona Arms

The **Madrona Arms** (☎206-739-5104; www.madronaarms.com; 1138 34th Ave; ⊗11am-midnight Mon-Fri, from 9am Sat & Sun; 🚍2) is fashioned in the old British tradition with obvious nods to Seattle (local draft ales). It's run by a Northern Irishman so there's Guinness on tap and some old-country food standards, including bangers and mash and shepherd's pie.

Explore
Capitol Hill & First Hill

Capitol Hill is Seattle's most unashamedly hip neighborhood, where the exceptionally rich mix with the exceptionally eccentric. While gentrification has let some of the air out of its tires, this is still Seattle's best crash pad for dive-bar rock and roll, LGBTIQ+ mirth and on-trend dining. More straitlaced First Hill is home to an art museum and multiple hospitals.

The Short List

○ **Pony (p106)** *Savoring sunset drinks on the patio that lead to all-night grinding on the dance floor at one of the city's most popular LGBTIQ+ bars.*

○ **Elliott Bay Book Company (p109)** *Spending an afternoon of lazy literary immersion at Seattle's most beloved bookstore.*

○ **Lost Lake Cafe & Lounge (p105)** *Enjoying a very late beer or a very early breakfast at the 24-hour Twin Peaks–themed Lost Lake Cafe.*

Getting There & Around

🚌 Metro bus 10 links Capitol Hill with downtown (Pine and 5th); bus 8 goes to the Seattle Center. To reach First Hill, catch bus 2 on the western side of 3rd Ave downtown and get off at the Swedish Medical Center.

🚋 The First Hill Streetcar links Capitol Hill and First Hill with the International District and Pioneer Square.

🚈 The Link light-rail line heads north to the U District and southwest to downtown (and, ultimately, Sea-Tac Airport) from Capitol Hill station.

Neighborhood Map on p104

Street corner in Capitol Hill CINECAM / SHUTTERSTOCK ©

Walking Tour 🚶

A Musical Education in Capitol Hill

*Capitol Hill vibrates most nights to the under-
ground sounds of Seattle. The neighborhood has
witnessed quite a few musical earthquakes over
the years. You won't find any stadium rockers
here, but you will find small, clammy pubs and
clubs providing an ideal pulpit for the best bands
and DJs you've never heard of.*

Walk Facts

Start Zion's Gate Records

End Baltic Room

Length 1 mile; two to four
hours

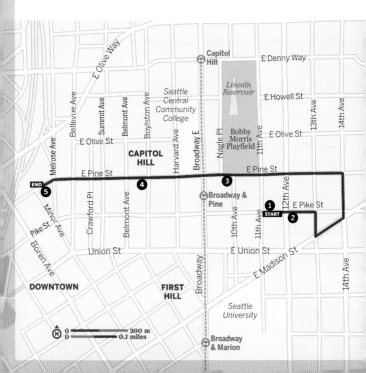

❶ Zion's Gate Records

While some record stores feel curated, **Zion's Gate Records** (📞206-568-5446; 1100 E Pike St; 🕐noon-8pm Sun-Thu, to 10pm Fri & Sat; 🚋First Hill Streetcar) is anything but. Of course, that's all part of the charm. Drop in ready to work your fingers, picking through records in search of rare LPs and 45s.

❷ Wall of Sound

Capitol Hill has more vinyl record stores than any other neighborhood. **Wall of Sound** (📞206-441-9880; www.wosound.com; 1205 E Pike St; 🕐11am-7pm Mon-Sat, noon-6pm Sun; 🚌10) is an old stalwart. It's tiny but absolutely loaded with great finds. It's the place to go in search of more obscure and unusual stuff.

❸ Century Ballroom

For something musically different, hit the **Century Ballroom** (📞206-324-7263; www.centuryballroom.com; 915 E Pine St; 🚋First Hill Streetcar) for a drop-in salsa or swing dance class (from $16). If you're already comfortable with your moves, you can skip the lesson and come on one of its dance nights to cut a rug in any number of styles (from $9, or included in the price of a class).

❹ R Place

The Hill is Seattle's primary gay-borhood and **R Place** (📞206-322-8828; www.rplaceseattle.com; 619 E Pine St; 🕐4pm-2am Mon-Fri, from 2pm Sat & Sun; 🚋First Hill Streetcar) is one of its most flamboyant but all-round welcoming perches – a pub-cum-club-cum-entertainment emporium. The action is spread over three floors. Stick to the ground floor if you like it low-key. Higher-up it gets progressively saucier with dancing, drag and bellowing karaoke.

❺ Baltic Room

Capitol Hill clubbers like the **Baltic Room** (📞206-625-4444; www.balticroom.com; 1207 Pine St; cover varies; 🕐9pm-2am Thu, 8pm-4am Fri & Sat; 🚌10) for its classy airs – luxuriously high ceilings, paper lanterns on the balcony, the works. But don't let that genteel description fool you: this is a place to let loose on the dance floor. Come for DJs spinning bumping tracks or the occasional live band.

Pike-Pine Corridor

The Pike–Pine corridor is where Capitol Hill matriculates when it's time to get out and about. You'll find more watering holes and danceatoriums here than you'll know what to do with.

N

0 ——————————— 400 m
0 ——————————— 0.2 miles

For reviews see
- ⊙ Sights   p105
- ✕ Eating   p105
- 🍸 Drinking   p106
- ★ Entertainment   p108
- 🏠 Shopping   p109

CAPITOL HILL

✕ 4
🏠 15

E Republican St

E Harrison St

E Thomas St

E John St

Capitol 🚇 Hill

E John St

E Olive Way

E Denny Way

E Denny Way

E Olive Way

Broadway & Howell

Cal Anderson Park

E Howell St

E Howell St

Seattle Central Community College

E Olive St

Bobby Morris Playfield

Pine St

E Olive St

🍸 2
9

E Pike St

Broadway & Pine

E Pine St

14 🏠
3 ✕

5 ✕

E Pike St

🍸 12

🍸 10

E Pike St

✕ 6

7 🍸

13 ★

E Madison St

E Union St

E Pike St

🍸 11

Broadway Ct

E Spring St

E Marion St

Broadway & Marion

Seattle University

E Columbia St

FIRST HILL

E Cherry St

1 ⊙
Frye Art Museum

James St

E Jefferson St

Seattle University

Sights

Frye Art Museum MUSEUM

1 MAP P104, B6

This small museum on First Hill preserves the collection of Charles and Emma Frye. The Fryes collected more than 1000 paintings, mostly 19th- and early-20th-century European and American pieces, and a few Alaskan and Russian artworks. Most of the permanent collection is stuffed into a rather small gallery and comes across as a little 'busy'; however, the Frye's tour de force is its sensitively curated temporary shows, which usually have a much more modern bent. (☏206-622-9250; www.fryemuseum.org; 704 Terry Ave; admission free; ⊙11am-5pm Tue, Wed & Fri-Sun, to 7pm Thu; P; 🚋First Hill Streetcar)

Eating

Sitka & Spruce MODERN AMERICAN $$$

2 MAP P104, A4

The king of all locavore restaurants, Sitka & Spruce was the pilot project of celebrated Seattle chef Matt Dillon. It has since become something of an institution and a trendsetter, with its country-kitchen decor and a constantly changing menu concocted with ingredients from Dillon's own Vashon Island farm. Sample items include house-made charcuterie and roasted-asparagus-and-liver parfait. Great choice for vegetarians too. (☏206-324-0662;

www.sitkaandspruce.com; 1531 Melrose Ave; plates $16-35; ⊙11:30am-2pm & 5-10pm Tue-Thu, to 11pm Fri, 10am-2pm & 5-11pm Sat, to 9pm Sun; 🖋; 🚌10)

Lost Lake Cafe & Lounge AMERICAN $

3 MAP P104, C4

It would be one thing if Lost Lake was merely a loving homage to David Lynch's hit TV mystery hour *Twin Peaks,* but the food is also fantastic – much better than other gimmick restaurants of its ilk. It specializes in diner grub, but sub in bold flavors and nix the frozen vegetables. Everything here is fresh and tasty. (☏206-323-5678; www. lostlakecafe.com; 1505 10th Ave; mains $12-15; ⊙24hr; 🚋First Hill Streetcar)

Coastal Kitchen MODERN AMERICAN $$

4 MAP P104, D1

Coastal Kitchen has become a local legend since its inception in

First Hill

First Hill, just south of the Pike–Pine corridor, is scattered with traces of Seattle's pioneer-era glory, including a few magnificent old mansions and some excellent examples of early Seattle architecture. First Hill is nicknamed 'Pill Hill' because it's home to three major hospitals.

2012 with its culinary theme (fish) and variations (a different geographical influence is introduced quarterly). Weekend 'blunch' is mega, as is the recently added oyster bar that complements the favorites: Dungeness crab cakes, Alaskan cod, Taylor shellfish and an epic sardine-heaped pasta. (206-322-1145; www.coastalkitchen seattle.com; 429 15th Ave E; mains $11-23; 8am-10pm; 10)

Cascina Spinasse   ITALIAN $$$

5 MAP P104, D4

Successfully re-creating the feel of an Italian trattoria, Spinasse specializes in the cuisine of northern Italy's Piedmont region. This means dishes like hand-cut egg noodles in a variety of appealing ragù sauces and pan-seared trout with Piemontese salsa. The finely curated wine list includes the kings and queens of the region's reds: Barolo and Barbaresco. (206-251-7673; www.spinasse.com; 1531 14th Ave; mains $26-45; 5-10pm Sun-Thu, to 11pm Fri & Sat; 11)

Frankie & Jo's   ICE CREAM $

6 MAP P104, C4

Frankie & Jo's is a 100% vegan ice-cream shop in Capitol Hill that specializes in lux flavors such as chocolate date, gingered golden milk and salty caramel ash, as well as made-from-scratch waffle cones. (206-557-4603; www.frankie andjos.com; 1010 E Union St; scoops $4-9; noon-11pm; ; First Hill Streetcar)

Drinking

Pony   GAY

7 MAP P104, C4

Pony (in a repurposed car garage from the 1930s) is the type of gay bar that has reached a level of popularity where most denizens of Seattle's LGBTIQ+ nightlife scene either absolutely love or loathe it. Come dance your brains out on a Saturday night or sip a beer on its patio on a sunny afternoon and decide for yourself.

This is definitely a gay dive and the music tends to skew toward indie pop, punk, disco and new wave. (206-324-2854; www.ponyseattle. com; 1221 E Madison St; 12)

Espresso Vivace at Brix   CAFE

8 MAP P104, B1

Loved in equal measure for its no-nonsense walk-up stand on Broadway and this cafe (a large retro place with a beautiful Streamline Moderne counter), Vivace is known to have produced some of the Picassos of latte art. But it doesn't just offer pretty toppings: many of Seattle's coffee experts rate its espresso shots as the best in the city. (206-860-2722; www.espressovivace.com; 532 Broadway E; 6am-11pm; ; Capitol Hill)

Victrola Coffee Roasters   CAFE

9 MAP P104, A4

Purveyors of a damned fine cup o' coffee since 2000, Victrola, to its credit, has clung to its grassroots, maintaining only four cafes. You can ponder how small is beautiful with one of its 4oz cappuccinos while watching the action in the roasting room. Come for the free 'cuppings' (a mix of a demonstration and tasting) with a coffee expert on Wednesday at 11am (www.victrolacoffee.com; 310 E Pike St; ⏰6:30am-8pm Mon-Fri, from 7:30am Sat & Sun; 🚊10)

Wildrose LESBIAN

10 🚊 MAP P104, C4

This small, comfortable lesbian bar has theme nights (Taco Tuesdays; karaoke on Wednesday starting at 9pm) as well as a light menu, pool and DJs. On weekends it gets packed, so expect a wait. (☎206-324-9210; www.thewildrosebar.com;

1021 E Pike St; ⏰5pm-midnight Mon, 3pm-1am Tue-Thu, 3pm-2am Fri & Sat, 3pm-midnight Sun; 🚊First Hill Streetcar)

Optimism Brewing Co MICROBREWERY

11 🚊 MAP P104, B4

Capitol Hill has lagged behind Fremont and Ballard beer-wise, but this encouragingly named brewery put froth back on the local pints when it opened in 2015. In the fine style of similarly oriented Fremont Brewing (p119), Optimism offers a tasting room where you can sit at picnic benches on the factory floor and order straight from the beer vat. (☎206-651-5429; www.optimism brewing.com; 1158 Broadway; ⏰noon-

Frankie & Jo's

STEFANO POLITI MARKOVINA / ALAMY STOCK PHOTOS ®

Elliott Bay Book Company

11pm Mon-Thu, to midnight Fri & Sat, to 9pm Sun; 👫 🐾 ; 🚋 First Hill Streetcar)

Entertainment

Neumos
LIVE MUSIC

12 ⭐ MAP P104, C4

This punk, hip-hop and alternative-music joint is one of Seattle's most revered small music venues. Its storied list of former performers is too long to include, but if they're cool and passing through Seattle, they've probably played here. The audience space can get hot and sweaty and even smelly, but that's rock and roll. (📞 206-709-9442; www.neumos.com; 925 E Pike St; 🚋 First Hill Streetcar)

Chop Suey
LIVE MUSIC

13 ⭐ MAP P104, D4

Chop Suey is a small, dark space with high ceilings and a ramshackle faux-Chinese motif. It serves burger-biased food as well as booze and music. The bookings are as mixed as the dish it's named after – electronica, hip-hop, alt-rock and other creative rumblings from Seattle's music underground. (www.chopsuey.com; 1325 E Madison St; ⏰ 4pm-2am Mon-Fri, 9pm-2am Sat & Sun; 🚋 12)

Shopping

Elliott Bay
Book Company   BOOKS

14 MAP P104, C4

Seattle's most beloved bookstore offers over 150,000 titles in a large, airy, wood-beamed space with cozy nooks that can inspire hours of serendipitous browsing. In addition to the size, the staff recommendations and displays of books by local authors make this place extra special. Bibliophiles will be further satisfied with regular book readings and signings. (206-624-6600; www.elliottbaybook.com; 1521 10th Ave; 10am-10pm Mon-Thu,

to 11pm Fri & Sat, to 9pm Sun; First Hill Streetcar)

Ada's Technical
Books & Cafe   BOOKS

15 MAP P104, D1

Ada's plush interior is done out in clean white wood with royal blue accents. There's a cafe on one side and a well-curated collection of books on the other (tech books are the specialty). Relax at the cafe tables or on a comfy chair in front of an old-fashioned fireplace. It also sells breakfast and sandwiches (mains $8 to $13). (206-322-1058; www.seattletechnicalbooks.com; 425 15th Ave E; 8am-9pm; 10)

Explore ⊕
Fremont & Green Lake

Fremont pitches young hipsters among old hippies in an unlikely urban alliance, and vies with Capitol Hill as Seattle's most irreverent neighborhood, with junk shops, urban sculpture and a healthy sense of its own ludicrousness. To the north, family-friendly Green Lake is a more affluent suburb centered on a park favored by fitness devotees.

The Short List

o **Fremont Public Sculptures (p112)** Walking around Seattle's most irreverent neighborhood in search of its peculiar public art, as well as keeping an eye out for any spontaneous 'art attacks.'

o **Woodland Park Zoo (p117)** Taking in chimps, giraffes, hippos and more at one of the better zoos in the US.

o **Green Lake Park (p117)** Joining the walking, running, skating, cycling mass of humanity powering around beautiful Green Lake Park.

Getting There & Around

🚌 Three different metro buses link Fremont to central Seattle. Bus 62 runs from downtown to Fremont. Bus 5 runs from downtown via Fremont to Phinney Ridge and Woodland Park Zoo. Bus 40 originates in downtown and makes stops along Fremont's N 36th St before breezing off to Ballard. For cross-town connections, buses 31 and 32 link Fremont with the U District.

Neighborhood Map on p116

Green Lake Park (p117) DAVID7 / SHUTTERSTOCK ©

Top Experiences 📷
Discover Fremont's Public Sculptures

Long known for its wry contrarianism, Fremont does bizarre like the rest of the world does normal. For proof, look no further than its public sculptures. The five most famous pieces are scattered around four square blocks in the southern part of the neighborhood abutting the Lake Washington Ship Canal.

🎯 MAP P116, D3

btwn N 34th St, N 36th St, Aurora Ave N & Evanston Ave N

admission free

🚌 5

Statue of Lenin

In 1993 Fremont's provocative bronze **statue of Lenin** (pictured; Map p116, C2; cnr N 36th St & Fremont Pl N; 🚌40) was salvaged from the people of Poprad (Slovakia). Given their resounding rejection of Soviet rule, they were probably glad to see the back of the bearded curmudgeon. It was unearthed by a resident of Issaquah, WA, named Lewis Carpenter, who found it unloved and abandoned in a junkyard while working in Czechoslovakia as an English teacher soon after the Velvet Revolution.

Fremont Troll

Just when you thought you had returned to planet earth, up sprouts the **Fremont Troll** (Map p116, D3; N 36th St & Troll Ave; 🚌62), a 13,000lb steel and concrete sculpture of a troll crushing a Volkswagen Beetle in its hand. It resides under the Aurora Bridge and does a good job of metaphorically guarding the neighborhood. The sculpture was the winner of a 1989 Fremont Arts Council competition to design some thought-provoking public art and has since appeared in films like *10 Things I Hate About You*. It took seven weeks to make.

Waiting for the Interurban

Seattle's most popular piece of public art, **Waiting for the Interurban** (Map p116, C3; N 34th St & Fremont Ave N; 🚌62), sculpted in recycled aluminum, depicts six people waiting for a train that never comes. The train that once passed through Fremont stopped running in the 1930s, and the people of Seattle have been waiting for a new train – the Interurban – ever since. (A new train connecting Seattle with Everett opened in 2003 but doesn't stop in Fremont.) The sculpture is prone to regular art attacks, when locals lovingly decorate the people in outfits corresponding to a special event, the weather, someone's birthday, a Mariners win – whatever.

★ **Top Tips**

o To get a more detailed and witty view of Fremont's sculptures, join the summer-only Fremont Tour (p117).

o After admiring the Fremont Troll, aim your camera south down Troll Ave. The massive concrete supports under the Aurora Bridge appear like the nave of a church.

✕ **Take a Break**

Just down from the Troll sits Fremont Brewing Company (p119), especially good in fine weather when half the neighborhood sits out front.

Pie (p115), just up from the guidepost, is snack heaven, whether your cravings are sweet or savory.

Walking Tour 🥾

Fremont Taste Tour

Fremont teems with microbusinesses all nurturing their own specialty, be it coffee, cider, beer, pies or chocolate. Some of the results never leave Fremont, meaning that outsiders have all the more reason to stop by to taste the flavors and – more often than not – meet the people who produced them.

Walk Facts

Start Pie

End Bad Jimmy's

Length 1 mile; one to two hours

❶ Pie

It's as simple as P-I-E. Bake fresh pies daily on-site, stuff them with homemade fillings (sweet and savory), and serve them in a cool, bold-colored Fremont cafe. The offerings at **Pie** (📞206-436-8590; www.sweetandsavorypie.com; 3515 Fremont Ave N; pies from $5.95; ⏱11am-7pm Mon-Wed, 11am-9pm Thu & Fri, 10am-9pm Sat, 11am-5pm Sun; 🚊5) are ideal for a snack lunch or you can double up and get a sweet one for dessert too. Broccoli cheddar and peanut butter cream are crowd pleasers.

❷ Fremont Coffee Co

A one-of-a-kind **coffee shop** (📞206-632-3633; www.fremontcoffee.net; 459 N 36th St; ⏱6am-8pm Mon-Fri, from 7am Sat & Sun; 🛜; 🚊40) in an old Craftsman-style house with art-adorned rooms and wicker chairs on a wrap-around porch. The clientele is hip-meets-hippie, and the coffee is refreshingly strong.

❸ Theo Chocolate Factory Shop

The **Theo Chocolate Factory** (📞206-632-5100; www.theochocolate.com; 3400 Phinney Ave N; tours $12; 🚊40) is both a thriving local business and one of Fremont's star tourist attractions (tours are given), but if you're just passing through and want to load up with a bit of the local flavor, swing by the onsite shop to stock up on its bitter-sweet chocolate.

❹ Outlander Brewery & Pub

A tiny microbrewery not quite small enough to be a nano-brewery, **Outlander** (📞206-486-4088; www.outlanderbrewing.com; 225 N 36th St; ⏱4-10pm Tue & Wed, 4pm-midnight Thu, 4pm-1am Fri & Sat, 2-10pm Sun; 🚊40) occupies the downstairs rooms of a creaky wooden house dating from the early 1900s and provides a cozy antidote to the crowded ebullience of other Fremont bars. It looks like someone's front room and probably was once.

❺ George & Dragon Pub

George & Dragon (📞206-545-6864; www.georgeanddragonpub.com; 206 N 36th St; ⏱11am-2am; 🚊40) is a friendly English boozer where the 'football' on TV is soccer and the 'chips' are rectangular, fried and not remotely French. The website has a schedule for upcoming games, as well as event nights like karaoke and painting parties.

❻ Bad Jimmy's

Follow the happy noises to this small taproom in a garage in the boxy warehouse district of West Fremont (or is it East Ballard?). Feeling more nano- than micro-brewery, **Bad Jimmy's** (📞206-789-1548; www.badjimmysbrewingco.com; 4358b Leary Way NW; ⏱3-10pm Mon-Thu, 3pm-2am Fri, noon-2am Sat, noon-10pm Sun; 🚶; 🚊40) specializes in strongly flavored ales – be they citrus, chocolate or even coconut – with high ABVs (your head will be swimming after one pint).

Fremont & Green Lake

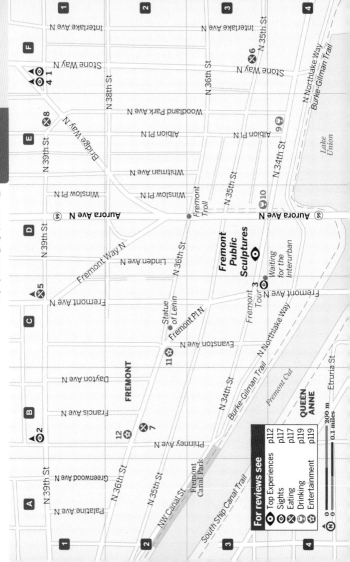

N Interlake Ave N
N Interlake Ave N
N Interlake Ave N

F
4 1

6

8

E
N 38th St
Bridge Way N

N 39th St
N 38th St
Stone Way N
N 37th St
N 36th St
N 35th St

Woodland Park Ave N
Albion Pl N
Albion Pl N
Whitman Ave N
Winslow Pl N
Winslow Pl N
N 34th St

Lake Union

9

D
N 39th St
Fremont Way N
Linden Ave N
N 36th St
Fremont Troll

Aurora Ave N
Aurora Ave N

10

Fremont Public Sculptures
Waiting for the Interurban

C
Statue of Lenin
Fremont Pl N
N Evanston Ave N
Fremont Ave N
Fremont Ave N

N Northlake Way
Fremont Tour
3

11

B
FREMONT
N Dayton Ave N
N Francis Ave N

5

N 34th St
Burke-Gilman Trail
Fremont Cut

A
N 39th St
N 36th St
Greenwood Ave N
N 35th St
Palatine Ave N

2

12
7
Phinney Ave N

NW Canal St
Fremont Canal Park
Fremont Canal Trail
South Ship Canal Trail

QUEEN ANNE
Etruria St

N Northlake Way

N Northlake Way
Burke-Gilman Trail

N 35th St
Stone Way N

N 36th St

N Northlake Way

Lake Union

For reviews see	
◉ Top Experiences	p112
◉ Sights	p117
⊗ Eating	p117
◑ Drinking	p119
✪ Entertainment	p119

200 m
0.1 miles

Sights

Green Lake Park   PARK

1 ◉ MAP P116, F1

A favorite hunting ground for runners, personal trainers and tattooed sunbathers, scenic Green Lake Park surrounds a small natural lake created by a glacier during the last ice age. The paths that wind around the lake are usually well used by those on foot and wheels of every variety, and make for some of the best people (and dog) watching in the city. (☏206-684-4075; 7201 E Green Lake Dr N; ⊙24hr; 🚌62)

Woodland Park Zoo   ZOO

2 ◉ MAP P116, B1

In Woodland Park, up the hill from Green Lake Park, this zoo is one of Seattle's most popular tourist attractions. Consistently rated as one of the top-10 zoos in the country, it was one of the first in the nation to free animals from their restrictive cages in favor of ecosystem enclosures, where animals from similar environments share large spaces designed to replicate their natural surroundings. (☏206-548-2500; www.zoo.org; 5500 Phinney Ave N; adult/child May-Sep $22.95/13.95, Oct-Apr $15.50/10.50; ⊙9:30am-6pm May-Sep, to 4pm Oct-Apr; 👪; 🚌5)

Fremont Tour   WALKING

3 ◉ MAP P116, C3

To help outsiders infiltrate Fremont's wacky underbelly, a group of enterprising locals have instituted the Fremont Tour, a 90-minute neighborhood stroll accompanied by outlandishly costumed guides with names such as Rocket Man and Crazy Cat Lady. (☏800-838-3006; www.thefremonttour.com; cnr N 34th St & Fremont Ave N; adult/child $20/free; ⊙Jun-Sep; 🚌62)

Green Lake Boat Rental   BOATING

4 ◉ MAP P116, F1

You can rent kayaks, canoes, paddleboats and stand-up paddleboards from March to October from the kiosk on the eastern shore of Green Lake (where there's also a cafe). (☏206-527-0171; www.greenlakeboatrentals.net; 7351 E Green Lake Drive N; per hour $24; ⊙9am-7pm May-Sep, weekends only Mar-Apr; 👪; 🚌62)

Eating

Paseo   CARIBBEAN $

5 ✖ MAP P116, C1

A glorified food shack whose overflowing Cuban sandwiches (which are a lot more generously stuffed than they are in Cuba) have long prompted plenty of Seattleites to reroute their daily commute in order to savor them. If you've come this far, you shouldn't overlook the exquisitely simple rice and beans either. (☏206-545-7440; www.paseorestaurants.com; 4225 Fremont Ave N; sandwiches $9.95-12.50; ⊙11am-9pm Tue-Fri, to 8pm Sat, to 7pm Sun; 🚌5)

The Whale Wins

EUROPEAN $$$

6 MAP P116, F3

Forget the whale: it's the sardines that are the main winners at this fish-biased restaurant that shares trendy Euro-style digs with the equally hip Joule restaurant next door. The sardines arrive on thick crispy bread spread with a heavenly mayo concoction and zesty veg. Indeed, the 'Whale' excels in veg. Have carrots and fennel ever tasted this good? (📞206-632-9425; www.thewhalewins.com; 3506 Stone Way N; small plates $12-16, mains $28-33; ⏰5-10pm Mon-Sat, 5-9pm Sun; 🚍62)

Revel

KOREAN $$

7 MAP P116, B2

This modern Korean-American crossover restaurant (with a bit of French influence thrown in) has quickly established itself as a big name on the Seattle eating scene thanks, in part, to its simple, shareable plates. Of note are the pork-belly pancakes, the short-rib dumplings and the various seasonal hot pots, all of which go down well with a cocktail or two. (📞206-547-2040; www.revelseattle.com; 403 N 36th St; small plates $12-19; ⏰check website; 🚍40)

Kamonegi

JAPANESE $$

8 MAP P116, E1

Tiny Kamonegi and its head chef and owner Mutsuko Soma are currently all the rage on the Fremont dining scene. The specialties here are soba noodles and tempura, and on the very vegetarian-friendly menu you'll find a satisfying selec-

Grizzly bear, Woodland Park Zoo (p117)

SCOTT WALMSLEY / SHUTTERSTOCK ©

tion of both. The restaurant feels refreshingly authentic down to its Tokyo side-street sized dining area (reservations strongly recommended). (☏206-632-0185; www. kamonegiseattle.com; 1054 N 39th St; mains $9-20; ⏰4-10pm Tue-Thu, to 11pm Fri & Sat; 🍴; 🚌62)

of a French sommelier. The 'bean menu' changes daily and, thanks to the expertise of owner Andrew Milstead, it rarely disappoints. (☏206-659-4814; www.milstead andco.com; 900 N 34th St; ⏰6am-6pm Mon-Fri, from 7am Sat & Sun; 📶; 🚌62)

Drinking

Fremont
Brewing Company   BREWERY

9 🚊 MAP P116, E4

This microbrewery, in keeping with current trends, sells its wares via an attached tasting room rather than a full-blown pub. Not only is the beer divine (try the seasonal bourbon barrel-aged Abominable), but the industrial-chic tasting room and 'urban beer garden' are highly inclusive spaces, where pretty much everyone in the 'hood comes to hang out at communal tables. (☏206-420-2407; www. fremontbrewing.com; 1050 N 34th St; ⏰11am-9pm; 👪🐾; 🚌62)

Milstead & Co   CAFE

10 🚊 MAP P116, D3

This fabulous neighborhood coffee bar in Fremont prefers to carefully select other people's beans rather than roast its own, but chooses them with the skill and precision

Entertainment

High Dive   LIVE MUSIC

11 ⭐ MAP P116, C2

A bit of a dive – but not an unpleasant one – this is one of two local live-music stalwarts in Fremont. It hosts rock primarily by small-name bands on their way up. Strong drinks and BBQ food provide the accompaniment. (www. highdiveseattle.com; 513 N 36th St; ⏰7pm-2am; 🚌40)

Nectar Lounge   LIVE MUSIC

12 ⭐ MAP P116, B2

This small and comfortable live-music venue in Fremont outgrew its humble beginnings to become a well-established club that includes a covered patio with stage views. It prides itself on hosting any genre of music and was an early refuge for hip-hop acts. Macklemore has played here. (☏206-632-2020; www.nectarlounge.com; 412 N 36th St; ⏰8pm-2am; 🚌40)

Walking Tour 🥾

Cheap Thrills on the Ave

The U District is like a little college town buried inside Seattle and 'the Ave,' aka University Way NW, is its heart, soul and (judging by the number of bars) liver. If you never stopped being a student, or just want to see how the college set lives, start at the southern end of 'the Ave' and work your way north.

Getting There

🚊 Light-rail connects the University of Washington to Capitol Hill and downtown

🚌 Metro buses 40, 31 and 32 will get you here from neighboring Fremont and Ballard.

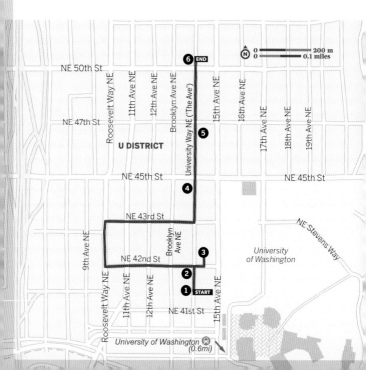

❶ Big Time Brewery & Alehouse

Big Time (☎206-545-4509; www.bigtimebrewery.com; 4133 University Way NE; ⏱11:30am-12:30am Sun-Thu, to 1:30am Fri & Sat; 🚌70) is one of Seattle's oldest brewpubs, conceived in 1988 – ancient history by microbrewing standards. During the school year it's crowded with students; for visitors, it's always a good barometer of the livelier side of life at the University of Washington.

❷ Aladdin Gyro-cery

Get in line behind tipsy undergrads and med students clocking out of their late-night hospital shifts at **Aladdin Gyro-cery** (☎206-632-5253; 4143 University Way NE; gyros $6-9; ⏱10am-2:30am; 🍴; 🚌70), where the gyros are greasy, filling and cheap.

❸ Cafe Allegro

You may not know it, but the **Allegro** (☎206-633-3030; www.seattleallegro.com; 4214 University Way NE; ⏱6:30am-9pm Mon-Fri, 7:30am-9pm Sat, 8am-9pm Sun; 🚌70) is a piece of history. Herein lies Seattle's oldest espresso bar in a 1975-vintage cafe that hasn't changed much since its pioneer days.

❹ Varsity Theater

For a look at where undergraduates go on their date nights, pop into the 1940s-era **Varsity Theatre** (☎206-632-2267; 4329 University Way NE; 🚌70), which shows a mixture of independent and international art-house films.

❺ Red Light

This U District thrift and vintage **shop** (☎206-545-4044; www.redlightvintage.com; 4560 University Way NE; ⏱11am-8pm Mon-Sat, to 7pm Sun; 🚌70) carries stylish and well-curated second-hand clothing. Think outlandish hats and dandy 'costumes' turned into modern-day fashion accessories. If you want to slip into life à la mode in Seattle, Red Light can get you outfitted.

❻ U District Farmers Market

Savvy Seattleites who can't abide the crowds of Pike Place hit the U District on Saturdays for this popular but not over-crowded **market** (5031 University Way NE; ⏱9am-2pm Sat; 🚌70). It's a food-only affair: all of its displayed produce comes from an alliance of 60-plus stall-holding farmers and is grown 100% in Washington State.

Explore
Ballard &
Discovery Park

A former seafaring community with Nordic heritage, Ballard still feels like a small town engulfed by a bigger city. However, that's not to say it's lacking in attractions. The neighborhood has come into its own as one of the city's best locales for exciting restaurants, lively bars and killer shopping.

Just across Salmon Bay is Discovery Park, one of the largest in the city and a must for those who love easy-to-tackle hikes ending in stunning views.

The Short List

o **Hiram M Chittenden Locks (p130)** *Feeling the breeze on your face and watching birds, fishing boats, motor yachts, kayaks and salmon negotiating the locks on a sunny summer's evening.*

o **Nordic Museum (p130)** *Learning about the history and culture of Ballard's most well-known immigrant community at this museum that received a major update in 2018.*

o **Discovery Park (p124)** *Feeling like you've left the city far, far behind in the verdant ocean-side oasis of Discovery Park.*

Getting There & Around

🚌 RapidRide D Line, which runs down 15th Ave NW, is the fastest direct bus into downtown. Metro bus 40 travels from downtown via Fremont to Ballard, stopping at multiple places in the neighborhood.

Neighborhood Map on p128

Top Experiences 📷

Go Wild at Discovery Park

A former military installation ingeniously transformed into a wild coastal park, Discovery Park is a relatively recent addition to the city landscape; it wasn't officially inaugurated until 1973. The largest green space in Seattle at 534 acres, its compact cornucopia of cliffs, meadows, dunes, forest and beaches stands as a healthy microcosm of the surrounding Pacific Northwest ecosystems.

◎ MAP P128, B6

📞 206-386-4236

3801 Discovery Park Blvd

admission free

🕐 4am-11:30pm

🅿️ 👪 🐾

🚍 33

Orientation & Trails

For a map of the park's trail and road system, stop by the **Discovery Park Environmental Learning Center** (⏰8:30am-5pm Tue-Sun) near the Government Way entrance. The main walking trail is the 3-mile **Loop Trail**, part of a 12-mile network of marked paths. Branch off onto the South Beach trail descending down a steep bluff if you want to view the still-functioning **West Point Lighthouse** (pictured), a great spot for panoramic views of the Sound and mountains to the west. You can circumnavigate back round to the Loop Trail via North Beach.

Seventeen acres in the north of the park are Native American land and home to the Daybreak Star Indian Cultural Center (p130), a community center for the United Indians of All Tribes Foundation (UIATF), a confederation of the many Native American tribes in the Seattle area.

Fort Lawton

The peninsula occupied by the park was originally Fort Lawton, an army base established in 1897 to protect Seattle from unnamed enemies. Fort Lawton didn't see much action until WWII, when it was used as barracks for troops bound for the Pacific theater. Over the course of the war it held up to 1400 German and Italian prisoners. When the fort was declared surplus property in the 1960s, the City of Seattle decided to turn it into a park, but various historic buildings from the fort remain.

Soon after the military officially pulled out in 2012, the old officers' houses, many of which date from the early 20th century, were refurbished for private sale. Because all 26 buildings are on the National Register of Historic Places, the exterior architectural features have been kept intact.

★ Top Tips

o There are half a dozen picnic areas in the park; the most scenic is next to the Daybreak Star Indian Cultural Center (p130).

o Discovery Park has five miles of paved bike trails.

✖ Take a Break

Discovery Park is wild – there are no food concessions or cafes. However, it's a beautiful place to have a picnic. If you're coming from Ballard, grab some sandwiches at Un Bien (p131). In Magnolia, the main shopping hub is on W McGraw St, between 32nd Ave W and 34th Ave W.

Walking Tour 🥾

Ballard's Bars & Beer Culture

Ballard's bars, breweries and pubs are almost a neighborhood in their own right. If you want the local gossip and unique libations of every stripe, this is where you should gravitate. Look out for historic, century-old bars, modern cocktail lounges, inventive brewpubs – massive to nano – and gastro-pubs with carefully configured retro decor.

Walk Facts

Start Jolly Roger Taproom

End Sunset Tavern

Length 1 mile; two to four hours

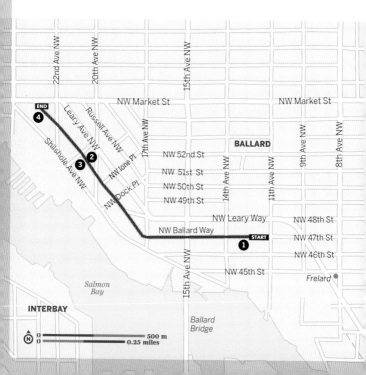

❶ Jolly Roger Taproom

A secret treasure tucked away off busy Leary Way, Maritime Pacific Brewing's **Jolly Roger Taproom** (☏206-782-6181; www.maritime brewery.com; 1111 NW Ballard Way; ⏲4-10pm Mon & Tue, 11:30am-11pm Wed-Sat, to 9pm Sun; 🚌RapidRide D Line) is a tiny, pirate-themed bar with a nautical chart painted on the floor. Choose from 15 different microbrews and sip away under a ceiling draped with pirate flags.

❷ Macleod's

Ballard's history was built on Nordic roots, but there are other 'northern' inflections to be found in Scottish-style pub **Macleod's** (☏206-687-7115; www.macleods ballard.com; 5200 Ballard Ave NW; ⏲4pm-midnight Sun-Thu, to 2am Fri & Sat; 🚌40). The extensive scotch and whiskey menu will leave connoisseurs flush with options and its fish-and-chips are some of the best in the city.

❸ King's Hardware

Ballard, like most of Seattle's neighborhoods, has changed a lot in the last couple of decades. To get a dose of some of the old-time grittiness borne out of its fishing-industry roots, decamp to **King's Hardware** (☏206-782-0027; www. kingsballard.com; 5225 Ballard Ave NW; ⏲3pm-2am Mon-Fri, from noon Sat & Sun; 🚌40), where the walls are loaded with taxidermy and the scuffed wooden benches reek of marinated beer.

❹ Sunset Tavern

The **Sunset Tavern** (☏206-784-4880; www.sunsettavern.com; 5433 Ballard Ave NW; ⏲bar from 5pm; 🚌40) is old-school Seattle at its finest. Its music calendar is filled with electrifying rock and folk acts that perform in the tavern's red-hued back room. Hang out up front for well-mixed cocktails and a chance to mingle with Ballard's most effortlessly cool denizens.

Frelard

The moniker 'Frelard' is sometimes used to describe the warehouse district where western Fremont dissolves into eastern Ballard, around Leary Way NW and 45th Ave. From the outside it looks like an abandoned industrial area, but it's replete with bars and breweries with new places opening all the time.

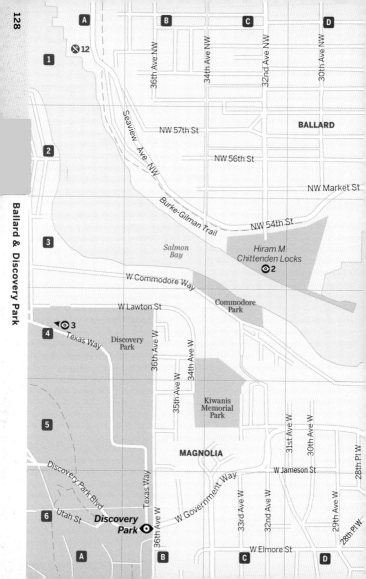

1
⊗12

A
B
C
D

36th Ave NW
34th Ave NW
32nd Ave NW
30th Ave NW

BALLARD

Seaview Ave NW

NW 57th St

2

NW 56th St

NW Market St

Burke-Gilman Trail

NW 54th St

3

Salmon Bay

Hiram M Chittenden Locks
◉2

W Commodore Way

Commodore Park

W Lawton St

◉3

4
Texas Way

Discovery Park

36th Ave W
35th Ave W
34th Ave W

Kiwanis Memorial Park

5

31st Ave W
30th Ave W
28th Pl W

Discovery Park Blvd

MAGNOLIA

W Jameson St

6
Utah St

Discovery Park ◉

Texas Way

W Government Way

36th Ave W

33rd Ave W
32nd Ave W
29th Ave W
28th Pl W

W Elmore St

A
B
C
D

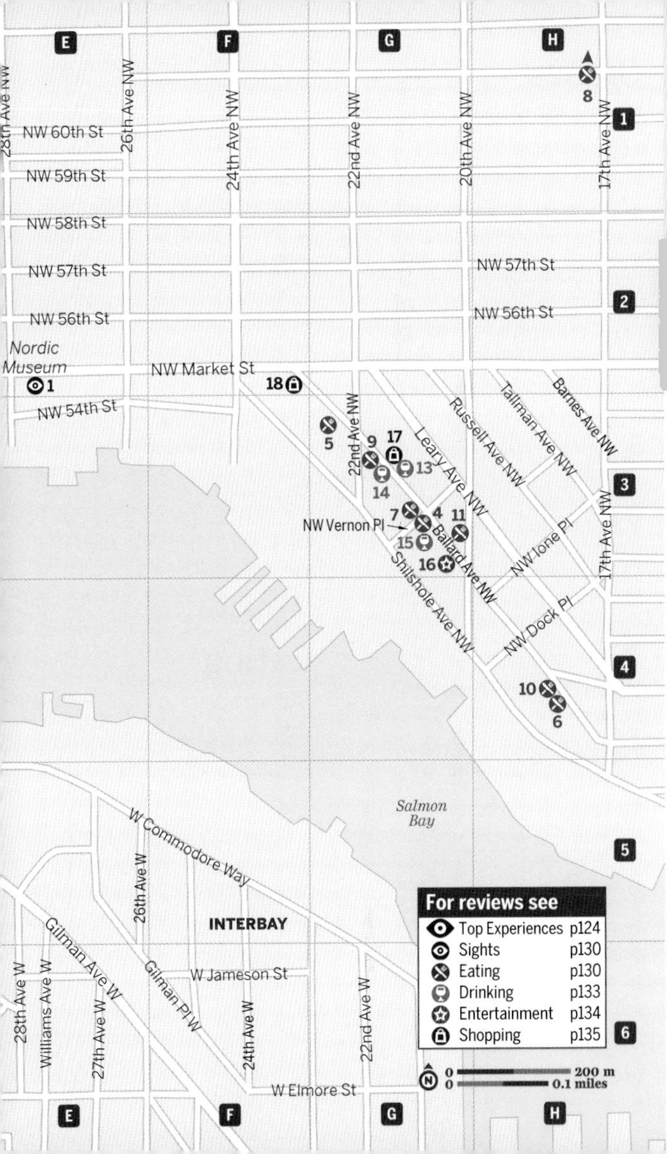

Ballard & Discovery Park

E | F | G | H

⊗ 8
1

NW 60th St
NW 59th St
NW 58th St
NW 57th St
NW 57th St
NW 56th St
2
NW 56th St

28th Ave NW
26th Ave NW
24th Ave NW
22nd Ave NW
20th Ave NW
17th Ave NW

Nordic Museum
⊙1

NW Market St
18 🔒

NW 54th St

⊗ 5

9 17 🔒
13
14

Barnes Ave NW
Tallman Ave NW
Russell Ave NW
Leary Ave NW

3

NW Vernon Pl →
7 ⊗
15
16 ✪

4 ⊗ 11
Ballard Ave NW

NW Ione Pl
17th Ave NW

Shilshole Ave NW

NW Dock Pl

4

10 ⊗
6

Salmon Bay

5

W Commodore Way

INTERBAY

W Jameson St

28th Ave W
27th Ave W
Williams Ave W
Gilman Ave W
26th Ave W
Gilman Pl W
24th Ave W
22nd Ave W

6

W Elmore St

🄽 0 ————— 200 m
0 ————— 0.1 miles

For reviews see	
⊙ Top Experiences	p124
⊙ Sights	p130
⊗ Eating	p130
🍺 Drinking	p133
✪ Entertainment	p134
🔒 Shopping	p135

E | F | G | H

Sights

Nordic Museum
MUSEUM

1 ◎ MAP P128, E2

Reason enough to come to Ballard – if the culinary scene and waterside parks weren't enough – is this delightful surprise of a museum dedicated to Nordic history and culture. In 2018 the museum upgraded in size from its original location in a historic schoolhouse to a newly constructed and fjord-inspired building. Its collections and temporary exhibits (usually an additional $5) represent a hugely accomplished collection of stories, artifacts and other assorted treasures from the recent and distant past. (📞 206-789-5707; www.nordicmuseum.org; 2655 NW Market St; adult/child $15/10; ⏰ 10am-5pm Tue, Wed & Fri-Sun, to 8pm Thu; P; 🚌 44)

Hiram M Chittenden Locks
CANAL

2 ◎ MAP P128, C3

Seattle shimmers like an impressionist painting on sunny days at the Hiram M Chittenden Locks. Here, the fresh waters of Lake Washington and Lake Union drop 22ft into saltwater Puget Sound. You can stand inches away and watch the boats rise or sink (depending on direction). Construction of the canal and locks began in 1911; today 100,000 boats pass through them annually. You can view fish-ladder activity through underwater glass panels, stroll through botanical gardens and visit a small museum. (3015 NW 54th St; admission free; ⏰ 7am-9pm; 🚌 44)

Daybreak Star Indian Cultural Center
CULTURAL CENTER

3 ◎ MAP P128, A4

Inside Discovery Park (p124) you'll find this cultural center that displays a permanent collection of Native American artwork and special exhibitions, and hosts events (check the online calendar). It's also a great place to pick up gifts – the on-site **Sacred Circle Gift Shop** (⏰ 10am-5pm Wed-Fri) is full of incredible indigenous art and crafts. (📞 206-285-4425; www.unitedindians.org; 5011 Bernie Whitebear Way; donations encouraged; ⏰ 9am-5pm Mon-Fri)

Eating

Bitterroot
BARBECUE $$

4 ✖ MAP P128, G3

People come to Bitterroot for two things: smoked meat and whiskey. Thankfully this restaurant with a pleasing modern roadhouse vibe does both exceptionally well. You can get your meat in sandwich form, or by itself with sides like cast-iron cornbread and roasted cauliflower. Likewise, the extensive whiskey menu comes neat or as an expertly mixed craft cocktail. (📞 206-588-1577; www.bitterrootbbq.com; 5239 Ballard Ave NW; mains $11-19; ⏰ 11am-2am; 🚌 40)

La Carta de Oaxaca MEXICAN $$

5 MAP P128, G3

La Carta de Oaxaca is easily one of Seattle's best lunch and brunch spots. Those who crave authentic Oaxacan-style cooking will swoon at the *birria* (braised leg of lamb) or the house special *mole negro Oaxaqueño* (chicken or pork in a chocolate and chili sauce). Whatever you order, expect serious flavors. (206-782-8722; www.lacartadeoaxaca.com; 5431 Ballard Ave NW; mains $11-18; 5-11pm Mon, 11:30am-3pm & 5-11pm Tue-Thu, to midnight Fri & Sat; 40)

Staple & Fancy ITALIAN $$$

6 MAP P128, H4

There's much to be said about Staple & Fancy's pedigree as another of Ethan Stowell's many hip Seattle eateries, but the bottom line is the food at this moody Italian restaurant is simply exquisite. Everything, from the seasonal cocktails to the perfectly al dente pasta, is imbued with well-balanced flavors and keen attention to detail. (206-789-1200; www.ethanstowellrestarants.com; 4739 Ballard Ave NW; mains $23-38, tasting menu $60; 5-11pm; 40)

Bastille Cafe & Bar FRENCH $$

7 MAP P128, G3

French but not at all faux, Bastille could easily pass for a genuine Parisian bistro if it weren't for the surfeit of American accents. First there's the decor: beautiful white tiles juxtaposed with black wood, mirrors and chandeliers. Then there's the menu: *moules* (mussels), *frites* (real French fries) and rabbit pâté, oysters and steak (all sourced locally). (www.bastilleseattle.com; 5307 Ballard Ave NW; mains $16-38; 4:30-10pm Mon-Thu, to midnight Fri & Sat, 10am-3pm & 4:30-9pm Sun; 40)

Un Bien CUBAN $

8 MAP P128, H1

Lines can get long at this Cuban take-out spot far from Ballard's

Seattle's Nordic Heritage

The bulk of Seattle's Nordic immigrants arrived in the late 19th and early 20th centuries and their appearance in the Pacific Northwest wasn't coincidental. The rain-sodden fjords, forests and mountains of Puget Sound coupled with the dominant industries of fishing and logging reminded the Scandinavian settlers of home. Nordics were instrumental in rebuilding Seattle after the 1889 Great Fire and were equally important in the early evolution of Ballard, then a separate city, and redolent of a Norwegian fishing settlement with its burgeoning salmon industry.

commercial center, but the wait is worth it to finally sink your teeth into a perfectly juicy and tangy pork sandwich. The restaurant is owned by brothers working from family recipes and you can taste the affection in every bite. (📞206-588-2040; www.unbienseattle.com; 7302 ½ 15th Ave NW; mains $11-16; 🕐11am-9pm Wed-Sat, to 8pm Sun; 🚌RapidRide D Line)

San Fermo ITALIAN $$

9 🍴 MAP P128, G3

San Fermo makes great use of its location in a historic single family home on Ballard Ave NW. It serves hearty Italian fare (think thick homemade noodles, buttery sauces and grilled branzino) for dinner and weekend brunch. While some changes have been made

to the home's interior, the rustic charm remains in the minimalist decorations and old-world design. (📞206-342-1530; www.sanfermoseattle.com; 5341 Ballard Ave NW; mains dinner $19-32, brunch $14-17; 🕐5-10pm Mon-Thu, to 11pm Fri, 10am-3pm & 5-11pm Sat, 10am-3pm & 5-9pm Sun; 🚌40)

Walrus & the Carpenter SEAFOOD $$

10 🍴 MAP P128, H4

Puget Sound waters practically bleed oysters and – arguably – there isn't a better place to knock 'em back raw with a glass of wine or two than here at the Walrus, a highly congenial oyster bar named not after a Beatles song but after a poem by Lewis Carroll

Ray's Boathouse

in *Through the Looking-Glass*. The accolades (like the customers) keep flying in. (📞206-395-9227; www.thewalrusbar.com; 4743 Ballard Ave NW; small plates $14-18; ⏰4-10pm; 🚌40)

Stoneburner   MEDITERRANEAN $$$

11 🍴 MAP P128, G3

Come and see homemade pasta prepared before your eyes in this popular restaurant affiliated with the swanky Hotel Ballard. Pasta-rollers massage dough at workstations in full view of the diners waiting to enjoy the fruits of their labor in Stoneburner's vaguely Parisian-style bistro. Pasta aside, the brunch breakfast pizza and creative vegetable dishes stand out. (📞206-695-2051; www.stoneburnerseattle.com; 5214 Ballard Ave NW; mains $18-34; ⏰3-10pm Mon-Thu, to 11pm Fri, 10am-11pm Sat, to 10pm Sun; 🚌40)

Ray's Boathouse   SEAFOOD $$$

12 🍴 MAP P128, A1

Out in western Ballard near the **Shilshole Bay Marina** (7001 Seaview Ave NW; 🚌44 from U District), Ray's is all about placid Olympic Peninsula views, nautical decor and an exhaustive fresh-fish menu. It offers tourists everything they imagine when they think about a nice dinner out in Seattle. (📞206-789-3770; www.rays.com;

Dining in Ballard

Ballard's restaurant scene is exemplary and always growing. Yes, the food is consistently impressive across the board, but it's the neighborhood's diverse dining options that really put it over the top. New American gastropubs, Mexican brunch spots, trendy Thai eateries and more crowd the neighborhood's commercial blocks. You won't want for a good meal while you're here.

6049 Seaview Ave NW; mains $28-46; ⏰5-9pm; 🚌44)

Drinking

Noble Fir   BAR

13 🍺 MAP P128, G3

Almost qualifying as a travel bookstore as well as a bar, Noble Fir's highly curated, hops-heavy beer list might fill you with enough liquid courage to plan that hair-raising trip into the Amazon, or even just a trek around Ballard. The bright, laid-back bar has a nook given over to travel books and packing cases on which to rest drinks. (📞206-420-7425; www.thenoblefir.com; 5316 Ballard Ave NW; ⏰4-11pm Wed & Thu, to midnight Fri, 1pm-midnight Sat, to 6:30pm Sun; 🚌40)

Little Tin Goods & Apothecary Cabinet
COCKTAIL BAR

14 MAP P128, G3

Even if you're not bowled over by the cutesy name you'll want to drop in for a unique and – most importantly – tasty cocktail at this Ballard hideaway. The interior is tastefully whimsical and feels like a secret garden miles away from the city outside. (808-635-6510; www.littletinballard.com; 5335 Ballard Ave NW; 5-11pm Wed & Thu, to midnight Fri & Sat year-round, noon-5pm Sun Apr-Oct, 4-10pm Sun Nov-Mar; 40)

Hattie's Hat
BAR

15 MAP P128, G3

As long as there's a Hattie's Hat, a bit of old Ballard will always exist. This classic old divey bar has been around in some guise or other since 1904. It was last revived with new blood in 2009 but hasn't lost its charm – a perfect storm of stiff drinks, fun-loving staff and cheap, greasy-spoon food. (206-784-0175; www.hatties-hat.com; 5231 Ballard Ave NW; 10am-2am Mon-Fri, 9am-2am Sat & Sun; 40)

Entertainment

Tractor Tavern
LIVE MUSIC

16 MAP P128, G3

One of Seattle's premier venues for folk and acoustic music, the Tractor books local songwriters and regional bands, plus quality touring acts. Music runs toward country, rockabilly, folk, bluegrass and old-time. It's an intimate place with

The Knocked Outs performing at the Tractor Tavern

Ballard Brewery District

If you've come to Seattle in search of good beer (smart move!) head directly to Ballard which, at last count, had 11 breweries, many of them conceived and ignited in the post-recessionary 2010s. There is even a name for the slice of neighborhood that most beer makers inhabit (roughly between 15 Ave NW and 8th Ave NW below NW Market St): the Ballard Brewery District.

a small stage and great sound; occasional square dancing is frosting on the cake. (☏206-789-3599; www.tractortavern.com; 5213 Ballard Ave NW; tickets $8-20; ⏲8pm-2am; 🚌40)

Shopping

Lucca Great Finds

GIFTS & SOUVENIRS

17 🔒 MAP P128, G3

One of the best things about this Ballard boutique is that it offers two shopping experiences: in the front is a chic PNW-themed home-wares store that will have you redesigning your apartment in your head while you browse, and in the back is a stationery shop with reams of enviably stylish wrapping paper and rows of charming greeting cards. (☏206-782-7337; www.luccagreatfinds.com; 5332 Ballard Ave NW; ⏲11am-6pm Mon-Fri, to 7pm Sat, 10am-5pm Sun)

Ballyhoo

ANTIQUES

18 🔒 MAP P128, F2

Even if you think you've been to every oddities shop worth a two-headed calf, Ballyhoo is worth a visit. What it lacks in space it makes up for in the breadth of its merchandise. On one side of the store you'll find fun trinkets in the $1 to $10 range and on the other a fossilized woolly mammoth tooth. (☏206-268-0371; www.ballyhooseattle.com; 5445 Ballard Ave NW; ⏲11am-8pm Mon-Thu, to 9pm Fri & Sat; 🚌40)

Explore

Georgetown & West Seattle

South of Seattle's city center, things are decidedly more mellow, but the neighborhoods here are full of unique attractions for curious visitors. The aptly named West Seattle area is teeming with cute commercial strips and some of the best parks and beaches in the city. To the east is Georgetown, an arty enclave hammered out of a former industrial district.

The Short List

○ **Museum of Flight (p138)** *Seeing how Homo sapiens got from the Wright Brothers to the Concorde in the space of just 66 years at this illustrious, entertaining and subtly educational museum.*

○ **Alki Beach Park (p141)** *Slowing down the rhythm a couple of notches on a weekend summer's afternoon on Alki Beach.*

○ **Georgetown (p143)** *Going on a pub crawl, or a vintage store crawl – or both – amid the redbrick bars and beer-stained history of this bohemian enclave.*

Getting There & Around

🚌 Metro buses 106 and 124 run frequently from downtown to Georgetown. The 124 carries on to the Museum of Flight. RapidRide C Line runs from downtown to West Seattle.

⛴ Hourly water taxis leave Pier 50 from the downtown waterfront to Seacrest Park in West Seattle. There's no weekend service in winter.

Neighborhood Map on p140

West Seattle SEASTOCK / GETTY IMAGES ©

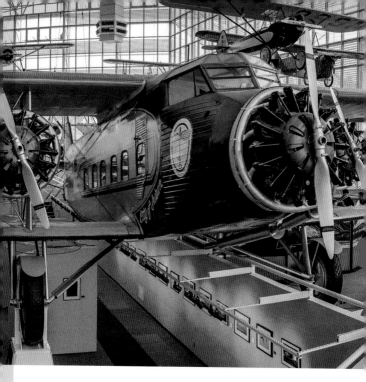

Top Experiences 📷
Dive Into Aviation History at the Museum of Flight

The city that spawned Boeing unsurprisingly houses one of the country's finest aviation museums, chronicling flight history from Kitty Hawk to Concorde. It includes exhibits on some of the most ingenious gravity-defying human-made objects: picture nefarious V2 rockets, Apollo lunar modules and gliders.

◎ MAP P140, C6

☎ 206-764-5720

www.museumofflight.org

Boeing Field, 9404 E Marginal Way S

adult/child $25/16

⊙ 10am-5pm, to 9pm 1st Thu of month

🕴; 🚍 124

Great Gallery

The centerpiece of the museum is a humongous gallery filled with historic aircraft that overhang chronological exhibits on the history of flight. If you're short on time, jump-cut to the **Tower**, a mock-up of an air traffic control tower overlooking the still-operational Boeing Field. Another must-see is a replica of the Wright Brothers' original 1903 *Wright Flyer*. Nearby, **X-Pilot simulators** pitch you into a WWII dogfight; they cost an extra $9 per person.

You'll also notice a significant part of the Great Gallery is devoted to space crafts. You can trace stories of starry voyages to the moon, Mars and beyond while studying life-size lunar modules, Viking landers and a replica of the research lab in the International Space Station.

Red Barn

Saved in the 1970s when it was floated upriver from its original location 3km away, this two-story red barn dating from 1909 was Boeing's original manufacturing space. It is filled with the early history of flight, with a strong bias toward the Boeing business.

Aviation Pavilion & Space Gallery

The Aviation Pavilion opened in 2016 and is accessible via a modernist bridge over E Marginal Way. It displays half a dozen iconic planes that you can look inside, including a British Airways **Concorde**; the first jet-powered **Air Force One**, used by presidents Eisenhower, Kennedy, Johnson and Nixon; and a **Boeing 727** prototype. The adjacent Space Gallery was built in 2012 to house the decommissioned **Full Fuselage Trainer** of the Space Shuttle. It costs an extra $30/25 per adult/child to explore the crew compartment.

★ **Top Tips**

o Entry is free on the first Thursday of each month from 5pm to 9pm.

o Ask at reception about free tours with an aviation expert (several times daily).

o For an extra $3 you can watch a flying-themed film in 3D in the on-site theater.

o Take a behind-the-scenes tours of the adjacent Boeing Field (Seattle's original airport). They run on weekends May to October and cost $25.

✕ **Take a Break**

Your best bet for refreshments is in the on-site Wings Cafe, overlooking the Boeing Field runways. It offers chunky sandwiches, salads, coffee and muffins.

★ **Getting There**

🚗 The museum is south of Seattle off I-5. There is ample parking on-site.

🚌 Metro bus 124 runs to the museum from downtown Seattle.

S Dawson St

A

B

C

D

1
SODO
S Dawson St
S Bennett St
S Brandon St

Denver Ave S
6th Ave S
5th Ave S

S Bennett St

S Lucile St

▼●◎⊗◎⊖
1 8 6 11

I-5

S Lucile St

S Dawson St

15th Ave S

S Findlay St

S Lucile St

15
🔒
2 ◎ Fogue Studios
& Gallery

BEACON
HILL

2
S Orcas St
S Mead St

Georgetown
Playfield

S Homer St
S Orcas St
S Fidalgo St

Corson Ave S

⊖
12

Airport Way S

3
6th Ave S

GEORGETOWN

S Front St

S Homer St
S Doris St 5 ⊗
14 ⊖
S Nebraska La
S Vale St 10 ⊗
S Harney St

18 🔒

12th Ave S

S Bailey St

13th Ave S

Airport Way S

Stanley Ave S

4
4th Ave S
5th Ave S

S Michigan St

5th Pl S
6th Ave S
7th Ave S

S Eddy St

S Albro Pl S Hardy St

7 ⊗

E Marginal Way S
S River St

5
13
16
▼
9
🔒
4 ▼
17
3 🔒

S Warsaw St

Corson Ave S
Carleton Ave S
Flora Ave S
Ellis Ave S

Boeing Field/
King County
International
Airport

6

S Willow St

E Marginal Way S

S Myrtle St

Museum of
Flight
◎

For reviews see	
● Top Experiences	p138
◎ Sights	p141
⊗ Eating	p141
⊖ Drinking	p143
🔒 Shopping	p144

Ⓝ 0 —————— 400 m
0 —————— 0.2 miles

A

B

C

D

Sights

Alki Beach Park

BEACH

1 ◎ MAP P140, C1

Alki Beach has an entirely different feel from the rest of Seattle: on a sunny day this 2-mile stretch of sand could be confused for California. There's a bike path, volleyball courts on the sand, and rings for beach fires. (206-684-4075; 1702 Alki Ave SW; 4am-11:30pm; 37)

Fogue Studios & Gallery

GALLERY

2 ◎ MAP P140, C2

This large gallery space is dedicated to the work of artists over the age of 50 and features a wide breadth of mediums – painting to pottery to abstract installations. (206-717-5900; www.foguestudios.com; 5519 Airport Way S; admission free; 11am-6pm Wed-Sat, noon-5pm Sun; 124)

Eating

Bakery Nouveau

BAKERY $

3 ✕ MAP P140, A5

No discussion of Seattle's best bakery omits Bakery Nouveau. The crumbly, craggy almond and chocolate croissants are as good as they get this side of the Atlantic. Don't take our word for it: the bakery consistently wins awards for its excellent pastries. (206-923-0534; www.bakerynouveau.com; 4737 California Ave SW; baked goods from $2; 6am-7pm Mon-Fri, 7am-7pm Sat, 7am-6pm Sun; RapidRide C Line)

Ma'Ono

HAWAIIAN $$

4 ✕ MAP P140, A5

The fried chicken sandwich – served on a King's Hawaiian roll with cabbage and a perfectly spicy sauce – at this West Seattle spot is one of the best things between two slices of bread currently available in Seattle. Treat yourself to one during the always-packed brunch, with a guava mimosa and a side of roasted sweet potato with caramelized lime. (206-935-1075; www.maonoseattle.com; 4437 California Ave SW; mains $12-17; 5-10pm Wed, Thu & Sun, 5-11pm Fri, 9am-3pm & 5-11pm Sat; 55)

Fonda la Catrina

MEXICAN $

5 ✕ MAP P140, C3

You'll find a number of things in the busy confines of Fonda la Catrina, a shockingly good Mexican restaurant in industrial Georgetown. There are the colorful Day of the Dead decorations and the Diego Rivera–inspired murals, strong drinks and – most importantly – fabulous food. (206-767-2787; www.fondalacatrina.com; 5905 Airport Way S; mains $9-14; 11am-10pm Mon-Thu, to 11pm Fri, 10am-11pm Sat, to 10pm Sun; 124)

Sunfish

SEAFOOD $

6 ✕ MAP P140, C1

You haven't really been to Alki until you've tried the fish-and-chips. Options include cod, halibut, salmon, fried oysters and clam strips – or combinations thereof. Sit at one

Finding Food in Georgetown and West Seattle

🍽️

While lighter on restaurant options than the city center neighborhoods, you'll find more than a few pleasant dining surprises in both West Seattle and Georgetown.

West Seattle has two separate eating nexuses: the seaside boulevard backing Alki Beach and the businesses spread along California Ave SW around the so-called 'Junction' with SW Alaska St.

Nearly all of Georgetown's eating joints are on or adjacent to Airport Way S.

of the outdoor tables and enjoy the boardwalk feel. (📞206-938-4112; 2800 Alki Ave SW; fish & chips $6-14; 🕐11am-9pm Wed-Sun; 👶; 🚌775 from Seacrest Dock)

Hangar Cafe
CAFE $

7 🍴 MAP P140, D4

No matter where you fall in the great 'sweet or savory' crepe debate, you're likely to enjoy the ones at Hangar Cafe. This extremely popular Georgetown eatery specializes in the French delicacy, but also has a large menu of sandwiches and salads. (📞206-762-0204; www.thehangarcafe.com; 6261 13th Ave S; mains $8-13; 🕐7am-3pm Mon-Fri, 8am-3pm Sat, to 2pm Sun; 🚌60)

Arthur's
AUSTRALIAN $

8 🍴 MAP P140, C1

Drop in at this sunny cafe in rainy Seattle for a taste of modern Aussie brunch food. We're talking big hunks of sourdough bread smothered in smashed avocado, thick-cut bacon and poached eggs, and marinated lamb sandwiches served with

pints of local beer. (📞206-829-8235; www.arthursseattle.com; 2311 California Ave SW; mains $10-14; 🕐9am-10pm Mon-Thu, 9am-11pm Fri, 8am-11pm Sat, 8am-10pm Sun; 🍴; 🚌55)

Itto's
TAPAS $$

9 🍴 MAP P140, A5

Settle in at this tiny, well-decorated restaurant and get ready to taste plate after plate of authentic Mediterranean and North African food, such as Moroccan lemon chicken and grilled squid steak in Romesco sauce. Sundays and Mondays, when bottles of wine are half off with purchase of food, are especially popular. (📞206-420-6676; www.ittostapas.com; 4160 California Ave SW; tapas $4-15; 🕐4pm-midnight Mon-Fri, from 2pm Sat & Sun; 🍴; 🚌RapidRide C Line)

Via Tribunali
PIZZA $$

10 🍴 MAP P140, C3

This small Seattle-founded chain operates in four of the city's hipper sanctums (including Capitol Hill and Fremont) plus a couple of foreign enclaves (NYC and Portland, OR). It deals not in pizzas but *pizze:* crisp-crusted Italian pies that are true to the food's Neapolitan roots. (☎206-464-2880; www.viatribunali.net; 6009 12th Ave S; pizza $15-20; ⏲11am-11pm Mon-Thu, to midnight Fri, 4pm-midnight Sat, 3-10pm Sun; 🚌124)

Drinking

West Seattle Brewing Co

MICROBREWERY

11 🚇 MAP P140, C1

The beer at the promenade-adjacent Alki Beach location of this popular microbrewery is fantastic, but it's the experience of sitting on one of the many lounge chairs facing the water and watching bikers and dog walkers go by that brings

the crowds. You'll have to fight for a spot outside on weekends; come on a weekday afternoon for maximum relaxation. (TapShack; ☎206-420-4523; www.westseattlebrewing.com; 2536 Alki Ave SW; ⏲3-9pm Tue-Fri, 1-9pm Sat & Sun; 🚌775 from Seacrest Dock)

Brother Joe

CAFE

12 🚇 MAP P140, C2

This trendy coffee shop mixes ultra-cool interior design (check out the giant gold faux-taxidermied rhino head and cat portraits on the wall) with a menu of interesting coffee drinks, such as the egg coffee (drip coffee, egg yolk and condensed milk). (☎206-588-2859; www.brotherjoegt.com; 5629 Airport Way S; ⏲7am-3pm Mon-Fri, 8am-2pm Sat & Sun; 🚌124)

Fonda la Catrina (p141)

Outwest Bar

GAY & LESBIAN

13 🚌 MAP P140, A5

Proof that you don't need to gravitate to Capitol Hill to enjoy a good gay-friendly neighborhood bar is this laid-back place with cocktails, burgers, DJs and regular karaoke. The vibe is friendly and casual and there are regular theme nights, such as Martini Monday and Lez Sing Wednesday (lesbian karaoke, natch). (☎206-937-1540; 5401 California Ave SW; ⏰4-10pm Sun-Tue, to midnight Wed & Thu, to 2am Fri & Sat; 🚌RapidRide C Line)

Jules Maes Saloon

BAR

14 🚌 MAP P140, C3

You could almost absorb the beer off the wallpaper in Seattle's oldest surviving pub: it's been serving since 1888, when the city was a youthful 37 years old. Once a speakeasy and allegedly haunted, it's a well-worn, comfortable, old-fashioned saloon with just the right contemporary touches: tattooed millennials at the bar, better-than-average food and a killer tap list of local microbrews. (☎206-957-7766; 5919 Airport Way S; ⏰11am-11pm Sun-Thu, to 1am Fri & Sat; 🚌124)

Shopping

Susan Wheeler Home

VINTAGE

15 🔒 MAP P140, C2

This newer addition to Georgetown's small vintage row manages to find a perfect balance of pleasingly cluttered yet artfully refined. There are shelves precariously stacked full of antique plates, tables covered in crystal glassware sets and an entire corner devoted to towels and linens from around the world. Somehow there isn't an item that doesn't feel specially selected. (☎360-402-5080; www.susanwheelerhome.com; 5515 Airport Way S; ⏰11am-6pm Wed-Sun; 🚌124)

Easy Street Records & Café

MUSIC

16 🔒 MAP P140, A5

Pearl Jam once played at Easy Street, arguably Seattle's most multifarious record store, and the business continues to sponsor regular events. Inside, young kids with elaborate tattoos mingle with graying ex-punks under a montage of retro parking signs

Easy Street Records & Café

URBANIMAGES / ALAMY STOCK PHOTO ©

Georgetown Second Saturday Art Attack

Georgetown's industrial art scene pulls together on the second weekend of each month at the Georgetown Second Saturday Art Attack (http://georgetownartattack.com/wordpress). This is the best time to visit the neighborhood's myriad galleries, some of which have rather sporadic opening hours. Almost the entire commercial strip takes part in the monthly event, which runs from 6pm to 9pm. Look for the free 'art ride' bus that runs up and down Airport Way S.

and Nirvana posters. Proving itself to be an invaluable community resource, Easy Street has its own cafe selling food, coffee and beer. (📞206-938-3279; www.easystreet online.com; 4559 California Ave SW; 🕓9am-9pm Mon-Sat, to 7pm Sun; 🚆RapidRide C Line)

Origins Cannabis
DISPENSARY

17 🔒 MAP P140, A5

Most dispensaries in Seattle have great customer service, but at this low-key West Seattle weed shop everyone is just an extra bit more friendly and attentive. If that weren't enough, it has a large selection with fun items like locally made edibles. (📞206-922-3954;

www.originscannabis.com; 4800 40th Ave SW; 🕓8am-11:30pm Mon-Sat, 9am-9pm Sun)

Georgetown Records
MUSIC

18 🔒 MAP P140, D3

This amazing record store had the guts to open in 2004 when vinyl sales were close to an all-time low. With the format now returning to its pre-1990s glory, it's an excellent place to score rare picture-cover 45s from obscure British 1970s punk bands (and plenty more). (📞206-762-5638; www.georgetown records.net; 1201 S Vale St; 🕓11:30am-8pm Mon-Sat, to 5pm Sun; 🚆124)

Survival Guide

Neon sign at Pike Place Market (p34)
CRACKERCLIPS STOCK MEDIA / SHUTTERSTOCK ©

Before You Go

Book Your Stay

◦ You'll typically find the cheapest hotel rates November through March.

◦ For good deals look outside of the city center neighborhoods and try places like Fremont, Ballard or West Seattle.

◦ Apartment rentals through services such as Airbnb are plentiful and inexpensive, but in some neighborhoods they may put you in the middle of the city's fight over gentrification. Research before you book.

◦ Parking is often extra, especially in the city center, and can cost up to $55 a night.

Useful Websites

Visit Seattle (www. visitseattle.org) Deals available through the 'Lodging' page of the official Seattle/King County website.

Seattle Bed & Breakfast Association (www. lodginginseattle.com) Portal of the city's 20

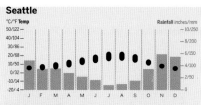

When to Go

◦ **Winter** Notorious for its dreary weather.

◦ **Spring** Plenty of rain with a few gorgeous days.

◦ **Summer** Dry, sunny and the best time to visit, but book ahead.

◦ **Fall** Weather is unpredictable, but the crowds thin out.

best B&Bs; check the 'Specials' page for info on packages and deals.

Best Budget

Moore Hotel (www. moorehotel.com) Cheap, historic and perfectly comfortable option on the cusp of downtown.

Hotel Hotel Hostel (www.hotelhotel.co) Fremont's only non-B&B accommodations – a kind of hipster hostel.

City Hostel (www. hostelseattle.com) Seattle hostel with private options and good wall art in Belltown.

Green Tortoise Hostel (www.greentortoise. net) Seattle's favorite backpacker haunt.

Best Midrange

Hotel Max (www. hotelmaxseattle.com) Boutique hotel with an art-and-music theme on the cusp of Belltown and downtown.

Moxy (http://moxy-hotels.marriott.com) Newer corporate boutique catering to tech business travelers with fun amenities and personable service.

University Inn (www. universityinnseattle. com) Close to the university, but a long way from austere student digs.

Palladian Hotel (www. palladianhotel.com) Big boutique hotel in Belltown with funky rock-star wall art.

Best Top End

Edgewater (www.edge waterhotel.com) Hotel steeped in rock history juts out over Elliott Bay.

Hotel Monaco (www. monaco-seattle.com) Lavish downtown hotel with refreshingly down-to-earth service.

Fairmont Olympic Hotel (www.fairmont. com/seattle) Seattle's jazz-age giant rolls out the red carpet in downtown.

Arctic Club (www. thearcticclubseattle. com) Commodious throwback to the age of the gold rush.

Arriving in Seattle

Sea-Tac International Airport

Light-rail connects the airport to downtown Seattle in 30 minutes. Shuttle buses stop on the 3rd floor of the airport garage and cost from $24.45 one way. Taxi fares start around $55 to downtown and take about 25 minutes.

King Street Station

King Street Station (Map p56, E4) is situated in Pioneer Square and on the cusp of downtown, and has good, fast links to practically everywhere in the city. Use light-rail to Westlake in the heart of downtown or take the streetcar to First Hill (both fares $2.25).

The Piers

Metro buses 24 and 19 connect Pier 91 in Magnolia with downtown via the Seattle Center. Fares are a flat $2.75. Shuttle Express links piers 66 and 91 with Sea-Tac International Airport ($34) or downtown ($22). Washington State Ferries dock at Pier 52 in downtown Seattle.

Getting Around

Bus

o Buses are operated by King County Metro Transit. Schedules, maps and a trip planner can be found on their website (http://kingcounty.gov/ depts/transportation/ metro.aspx).

o All bus fares within Seattle city limits are a flat $2.75. Those aged six to 18 pay $1.50, kids under six are free, and seniors and travelers with disabilities pay $1.

o Be aware that very few buses operate between 1:30am and 5am.

Streetcar

o There are two streetcar lines: the South Lake Union line, which runs between the Westlake center and Lake Union, and the First Hill line, which runs from Pioneer Square to Capitol Hill.

o Fares on both lines are a standard $2.25/1.50 per adult/child.

o Both lines run roughly every 15 minutes from 5am to 1am (10am–8pm Sundays and holidays).

Light-Rail

o Runs from Sea-Tac Airport to the University of Washington via Westlake Station in downtown. Stations include SoDo, the International District, Pioneer Square and Capitol Hill.

• Fares within the city limits are $2.25. From downtown to the airport costs $3.

Car & Motorcycle

• Seattle traffic is disproportionately heavy and chaotic for a city of its size; driving downtown is best avoided if at all possible.

• To rent a car, you need a valid driver's license and a major credit card. If you are traveling from overseas and your license is not in English, it is recommended that you get an International Driving Permit (IDP).

Bicycle

• Seattle and all of King County require that cyclists wear helmets. If you're caught without one, you can be fined $30 to $80 on the spot.

• There are plenty of bike rental operations around the city (most include helmets with your rental).

• Get a copy of the Seattle Bicycling Guide Map, available at most bike shops or by download (www.cityofseattle.net/transportation/bike maps.htm).

Taxi

• All Seattle taxi cabs operate at the same rate, set by King County. At the time of writing the rate was $2.60 at meter drop, then $2.50 per mile. You may incur additional charges for extra passengers or baggage. They can be hailed from the street, but it's safer order one.

• Services like Uber and Lyft are prevalent.

Boat

A water taxi connects the downtown waterfront (Pier 50) with West Seattle (Seacrest Park). It runs hourly every day in summer and weekdays only in winter. The fare is $5.75 .

Essential Information

Accessible Travel

All public buildings (including hotels, restaurants, theaters and museums) are required by law to provide wheelchair access and to have appropriate restroom facilities available. Phone companies provide relay operators for the hearing impaired. Dropped curbs are standard at intersections throughout the city.

Around 80% of Metro buses are equipped with wheelchair lifts. Timetables marked with an 'L' indicate wheelchair accessibility. Let the driver know if you need your stop to be called and, if possible, pull the cord when you hear the call. Service animals are allowed on Metro buses. Passengers with disabilities qualify for a reduced fare but first need to contact **Metro Transit** (☏ 206-553-3000; http://kingcounty.gov/depts/transportation/metro.aspx) for a permit.

Most large private and chain hotels have suites for guests with disabilities. Many car-rental agencies offer hand-controlled models at no extra charge. Make sure you give at least two days' notice. All major airlines, Greyhound buses and Amtrak trains often sell two-for-one packages when attendants of passengers with serious disabilities are required. Download Lonely Planet's free Accessible Travel guides from http://lptravel.to/AccessibleTravel.

Business Hours

Banks 9am or 10am to 5pm or 6pm weekdays; some also 10am to 2pm Saturday with many other businesses having the same hours.

Shops 9am or 10am to 5pm or 6pm (or 9pm in shopping malls) weekdays, noon to 5pm (later in malls) weekends; some places open till 8pm or 9pm

Discount Cards

If you're going to be in Seattle for a while and plan on seeing its premier attractions, consider buying a **Seattle CityPASS** (www.citypass.com/seattle; adult/child $99/79). Good for nine days, the pass gets you entry into five sights: the Space Needle, Seattle Aquarium, Argosy Cruises Seattle Harbor Tour, Museum of Pop Culture *or* Woodland Park Zoo, and Pacific Science

Center *or* Chihuly Garden & Glass.

Electricity

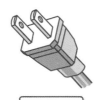

Type A
120V/60Hz

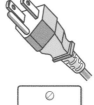

Type B
120V/60Hz

LGBTIQ+ Travelers

Seattle is a progressive, liberally minded city with thriving communities across the spectrum of sexual and gender identities; estimates are that approximately 13% of the city's population identifies itself as a member of the broader LGBTIQ+ community. While LGBTIQ+ people may face discriminatory attitudes, as they might elsewhere in the US, the city's population as a whole is known for generally welcoming attitudes toward sexual orientations and gender identities other than their own.

Money

Seattle is a very accessible city as far as money is concerned. Most businesses accept credit and debit cards and there are easy-to-access ATMs and banks everywhere.

ATMs

ATMs are easy to find: there's practically one per block in the busier commercial areas, as

Dos & Don'ts

In true West Coast tradition, Seattle is a casual city.

○ Dressing up for dinner is the exception rather than the rule. In the birthplace of grunge, shirts and ties aren't common and you'll rarely be turned away from somewhere for being inappropriately dressed.

○ For a large city, Seattle is a noticeably friendly place. Expect to strike up conversations in bars or lines.

○ Aggressive driving is frowned upon and Seattleites only honk their horns for emergencies. Even jay walking is likely to attract some dirty looks.

well as one outside every bank. Many bars, restaurants and grocery stores also have machines, although the service fees for these can be steep ($2 to $4, plus your own bank's fees).

Changing Money

Banks and money-changers will give you US currency based on the current exchange rate.

Credit & Debit Cards

Major credit cards are accepted at most hotels, restaurants and shops throughout Seattle. Be sure to confirm with your bank before you leave that your debit card will be accepted in other states or countries. Debit cards from large commercial banks can often be used worldwide.

Tipping

Tipping is a way of life in the US and not optional.

Bartenders and wait-staff 18% to 25%

Hotel porters $1 to $3 per bag

Hotel maids $2–5 a day (left out in room)

Taxi drivers 18% to 20%

Public Holidays

National public holidays are celebrated throughout the USA. On public holidays, banks, schools and government offices (including post offices) are closed and public transportation follows a Sunday schedule. Plan ahead if you're traveling – during many public holidays flights are full, highways are jammed and on Christmas and Thanksgiving, many grocery stores and restaurants close for the day.

New Year's Day January 1

Martin Luther King Jr Day Third Monday in January

Presidents' Day Third Monday in February

Memorial Day Last Monday in May

Independence Day July 4

Labor Day First Monday in September

Indigenous People's Day Second Monday in October

Veterans' Day November 11

Thanksgiving Day
Fourth Thursday in
November

Christmas Day
December 25

Responsible Travel

Ditch the car. Seattle has an extensive and easy-to-use public transportation network. Skip renting a car or relying on taxis and you'll avoid contributing to the city's notorious traffic.

Buy Native. Support Seattle's Indigenous communities by patronizing their businesses. Whether you're looking to buy traditional arts and crafts or to sample contemporary Native American cuisine, visit intentionalist.com for a directory of Native-owned businesses in the city. Visit with compassion. Consider making a donation to a charity working to combat Seattle's homelessness crisis, such as Facing Homelessness or Mary's Place. Treat unhoused people with common courtesy.

Safe Travel

COVID-19 safety protocols, including mask mandates and proof of vaccination or negative test requirements to enter certain businesses, are liable to change. Even if mandates have been lifted, individual businesses may still require masking at their discretion. Check www.seattle.gov/covid-19 for Seattle COVID-19 advisories and www.cdc.gov/coronavirus for travel requirements.

Smoking

Washington State law prohibits smoking in, or within 25ft of, all public buildings. Most state and private smoking policies also prohibit vaping.

Toilets

Public toilets abound in Seattle. You'll find them most readily in shopping malls and public parks. They are nearly always free of charge. If you're in a pinch, buy something in one of the city's many coffee shop and use their facilities.

Tourist Information

Visit Seattle (Map p40, E2; ☏ 206-461-5800; www.visitseattle.org; 701 Pike St, Downtown; ☺ 9am-5pm daily Jun-Sep, Mon-Fri Oct-May; ☒ Westlake) The main tourist information center is in the Washington State Convention Center in downtown.

Visas

Visa requirements vary widely for entry to the US and are liable to change; check www.travel.state.gov for up-to-date information.

Behind the Scenes

Send Us Your Feedback

We love to hear from travelers – your comments help make our books better. We read every word, and we guarantee that your feedback goes straight to the authors. Visit **lonelyplanet.com/contact** to submit your updates and suggestions.

Note: We may edit, reproduce and incorporate your comments in Lonely Planet products such as guidebooks, websites and digital products, so let us know if you are happy to have your name acknowledged. For a copy of our privacy policy visit **lonelyplanet.com/legal**.

Robert's Thanks

Thank you, as always, to my friends and family for your continued support while I run hither and thither and yon. Special thanks to Karin, for sharing your love of Seattle with me and setting me off on the right foot, and to Lynae for the wonderful home away from home where I made many great memories.

Acknowledgements

Front cover photograph: Space Needle and Museum of Pop Culture, Getty Images/Naeem Jaffer © (Museum of Pop Culture by Gehry Partners, LLP.). Back cover photograph: Pike Place Public Market, Shutterstock/cdrin ©.

This Book

This third edition of Lonely Planet's *Pocket Seattle* guidebook was researched, written and curated by Robert Balkovich. The first edition was researched and written by Brendan Sainsbury. This guidebook was produced by the following:

Destination Editor
Ben Buckner

Senior Product Editors
Sasha Drew, Grace Dobell, Martine Power

Cartographers
Julie Sheridan, Valentina Kremenchutskaya, Alison Lyall

Product Editors Damian Kemp, Barbara Delissen, Kathryn Rowan

Book Designers Nicolas D'Hoedt, Fergal Condon

Assisting Editors Sarah Bailey, James Bainbridge, Carly Hall, Gabby Innes, Lou McGregor, Monique Perrin

Cover Researcher
Lauren Egan

Thanks to Ronan Abayawickrema, Sonia Kapoor, Andi Jones, Amy Lynch, Lauren O'Connell, Charlotte Orr

Index

See also separate subindexes for:

⊗ Eating p157
◐ Drinking p158
✪ Entertainment p159
🔒 Shopping p159

✪ Entertainment

🛍 Shopping

Our Writer

Robert Balkovich

Robert was born and raised in Oregon, but has called New York City home for almost a decade. When he was a child and other families were going to theme parks and grandma's house, he went to Mexico City and toured Eastern Europe by train. He's now a writer and travel enthusiast seeking experiences that are ever so slightly out of the ordinary to report back on. Instagram: oh_balky

Published by Lonely Planet Global Limited
CRN 554153
3rd edition – Nov 2022
ISBN 978 1 78868 449 1
© Lonely Planet 2022 Photographs © as indicated 2022
10 9 8 7 6 5 4 3 2 1
Printed in Singapore

Although the authors and Lonely Planet have taken all reasonable care in preparing this book, we make no warranty about the accuracy or completeness of its content and, to the maximum extent permitted, disclaim all liability arising from its use.